THINK TO WIN

THINK TO WIN

John Syer and
Christopher Connolly

S I M O N   &   S C H U S T E R

LONDON·SYDNEY·NEW YORK·TOKYO·SINGAPORE·TORONTO

First published in Great Britain by
Simon & Schuster Ltd in 1991
A Paramount Communications Company

Simon & Schuster Ltd
West Garden Place
Kendal Street
London W2 2AQ

Simon & Schuster of Australia Pty Ltd
Sydney

A CIP catalogue record for this book is
available from the British Library
ISBN 0–671–69717-X

Typeset in Plantin 10.5/12.5 by Selectmove Ltd
Printed and bound in Great Britain by
Billing & Sons Ltd, Worcester

Contents

ACKNOWLEDGMENT

We particularly wish to thank Dr. Piero Ferrucci for giving us permission to include several quotations that originally appeared in his well-researched book *Inevitable Grace*.

Change, Discovery and Thinking to Win

The challenge of change

This book invites you to discover your current patterns of behaviour, a dangerous step perhaps because awareness invites change. As you discover what you actually do, you become aware of a new vision of what you might be able to achieve.

You are then presented with a great challenge: can you let go of these familiar patterns? Few of us find this easy. Change can be threatening, even when you know that it leads to a winning position. And change is often more difficult, the older and more experienced you are.

The implications of change can be mind-boggling whether at a professional or personal level. If you work in a monolithic organisation or even a medium-sized national body, surrounded by colleagues and superiors who hold on tight, giving little overt responsibility, you are likely to become entrenched yourself. Anyone, from the telephone operators to top management, can feel threatened in such circumstances. It is natural to feel trapped and defensive. In such an organisation, there is a tremendous temptation to stick tight to the rules in the face of even the most persuasive argument and hang on grimly to what little power and control you have gained.

If you make this mistake you are not alone. It's not so very long ago that whole business organisations suffered through

refusing to change. Kodak and Xerox lost a major share of
their market to foreign competitors in the late 1970s in this
way and the whittling down of the British Leyland and Austin
automobile empires are similar examples. General Motors, for
years the largest corporation in the world, fell into the same trap
and failed disastrously in 1986 and 1987. In the sports world
too, those sports with the longest and proudest traditions too
often find that the legacy of the past creates a barrier to new
growth and ideas.

If sports administration has its difficulties, so to do managers
and coaches. In the eyes of many, England ceased to be a major
force in international soccer until the 1990 World Cup. This
too was blamed on a dogged retention of a formula that had
proved successful in the past. Until 1990, when a combination
of accident and design showed the possibility of change, the
English game had long been heads down, graft and 'do what I
say'. No team, no individual can change nothing and grow at
the same time.

This is also true of our personal relationships. Fear of
the unknown leaves many of us stagnating in 'compromise'
situations. We are frightened to take the plunge and alter our
everyday, familiar routines, even when we know that the result
will be better for everyone all round.

Change is the key to growth and improved performance
in every aspect of our lives. This psychological principle is
now appreciated by most of the business world. In fact, in
forward-looking businesses, change is recognised as the only
constant.

The way to change

This book can help you find new ways of expressing your
potential, developing an openness to change as a constant.
By clarifying your 'vision' and becoming acutely aware of
your current situation, you will learn how best to respond to
the present moment.

Your personal plan will involve recognising the nature of your present situation, re-evaluating your understanding of it, letting go of old, unproductive patterns of action, introducing new approaches and practices, and then establishing ways of maintaining the new behaviour.

Discover more about yourself

Self-discovery inevitably improves your performance, particularly in the long-term. Reading this book will help you to optimalise your ability in your chosen field, be it sport, business, commerce, arts, education or whatever and attain mental fitness without resorting to chemical substances or the manipulation of others. Even those who suspect winning is dangerous or believe that winning is wrong will find something here.

In our vocabulary, winning and success are allied to discovery. Even where there are contestants, the one who wins the competition is not always 'the winner': 'the loser' may learn more. If I'm a mountaineer who scales a peak for the first time I have certainly won whilst competing against no-one but myself. For us there is a deeper significance to winning, unrelated to beating an opponent. To win is to discover more about oneself and to find a more complete mode of self-experience.

Competition can be 'neurotic' or 'creative'. As a neurotic competitor you are out to prove that you are something you believe you should be, or that others have told you to be, at the expense of opponents whom you consider to be of lesser worth if you beat them. By contrast, as the creative competitor, you compete to discover new aspects of your ability against an opponent whom you honour in the knowledge that, but for this challenge, you would have no such opportunity. Indeed you come to recognise that together, you and your opponent can achieve a level of understanding that neither of you could achieve without the other.

Winning does not apply solely to the sports field. Our first book *Sporting Body, Sporting Mind: An Athlete's Guide to Mental Training* was addressed to athletes and written when we specialised in mental training for sports people. Yet, as soon as it was published in May 1984, we were approached by Scandinavian Airline Systems with a request that we apply our programme to the performance of in-flight crews. As other business clients followed, we realised that the similarities between sport and business are legion. Both require the mental skills of concentration, confidence, motivation and the ability to deal with stress, both have teams and both have leaders – only the technical and physical requirements are different.

Similar skills are required in other areas of life. Perhaps you teach or build, act or design, fly aeroplanes or sell stamps. If so, you may not consider yourself a competitor at all and may even believe winning is wrong. Yet you do interact with others and have to meet the challenge of ensuring such interactions are effective if your own performance is to be a success. Even if your occupation is quite self-contained, you have to set yourself targets and meet them successfully if you are to optimalise your ability. Reaching any meaningful target involves overcoming obstacles along the way. For us, negotiating these obstacles successfully means that you win.

Time for change

Use this book when you decide it is time to step back and assess your performance. You may do this because you are in the grip of a mid-life crisis and you feel your career is at a crossroads. You may stop for a moment just to gain breath, to check your bearings before charging back into the fray. Or you may just have noticed that you've been doing the same thing, acting out the same patterns, for too long and feel you are in a rut.

If it is time for you to get in touch with the source of your faith and inspiration, this book will help. However, you must *interrupt* your performance and take stock. For a while you are invited to become an observer, a judge and a teacher. You are invited to make some change.

This book can help you to restructure your performance entirely or it can be used as a reference book, a book that suggests how to improve a particular skill or aspect of your performance as a whole.

Thinking to win

When we started out on a five-year period of work for Tottenham Hotspur Football Club in October 1980, Keith Burkinshaw the manager asked how he should introduce us to the lads. 'Well', one of us said, 'as sports psychologists, I suppose.' 'No', said Keith, 'I can't call you psychologists, they'd get the wrong idea. They'd think you were there to analyse them.' 'Okay', we replied, 'then how about mental trainers'. Keith laughed out loud at that. 'Come on. I can't call you *mental* now, can I?' And he introduced us as 'John and Chris'.

Since that time, however, our term 'mental training' has become relatively common, even if its definition sometimes deviates from our own. For us, mental training is using your mind to improve your performance. Hence, the title of this book: *Think to Win*.

We think in two different ways, ways which correspond to the use of the two hemispheres of the brain. Left-brain thinking is logical and analytical, thoughts usually being expressed in words. Right-brain thinking is associative and intuitive, thoughts often being expressed in images, pictures or musical sound. In this book we call these two types of thought 'thinking about' (analysing) and 'thinking of' (imaging).

Mental training involves both types of thought, both sides of the brain, and is a set of mental exercises that may be used to improve physical, technical and mental performance. The same or similar exercises may be used to improve your performance in any sphere of life. This book shows you how.

The strategy

The first step is to focus on where you wish to be or what you want to attain. For this you need a personal Vision and specific goals. We describe a process that we've developed considerably since starting work with the Ford Motor Company in March 1987. Equally applicable to individuals or teams, it will serve as a guide whether you are making radical changes to your life or developing a specific personal skill.

Discovering your Vision, like climbing a steep hillside, takes time and effort but is equally exhilarating. This is a major exercise in gaining perspective and one we would urge you to do if you feel you have been caught up in the demands of your daily routine for too long. The more pressured you feel, the more likely it is that you should take time to get a perspective, to reaffirm where you want to be in relation to where you are now.

Once you have your Vision and set your goals, you are free to focus on immediate plans. What are your first steps to be? Where do you want to be in a month from now and what particular skills do you want to have improved by then? The next chapter, entitled 'Where you are now?' helps you clarify this.

Whatever your Vision, you will have both inner and outside resources to help achieve it and also inner and outside obstacles in your path. In the following chapters, you will discover techniques for eliminating or 'reframing' the obstacles, and techniques for maximising your resources.

The last part of the book is for reference, providing a more detailed explanation of mental training and the process for change. Chapter 9 begins with an explanation of the scope of mental training (as compared to that of physical or technical training) and continues with an outline of the various phases of preparation – long term, preparation on the day and preparation at intervals throughout your performance. This chapter ends with a list of guidelines for building a mental training programme. Chapter 10 is a description of all the mental training exercises you might draw on when composing your plan of action, whilst Chapter 11 gives an in-depth account of the five stages of change – awareness, disidentification, reframing, re-creation and synthesis – through which you will have travelled on your way to your goal. The book ends with three case studies which illustrate the entire process.

If, having read this book, you would like to know more about our work with individual and team performance, please write to us at

Sporting Bodymind Ltd.
18 Kemplay Road
London NW3 1SY

Tel: (071) 794 4066
Fax: (071) 794 6700

1
Visioning: the pathway to success

We are all visionaries. Each of us has dreams of how the future might be. Already in childhood we have fantasies of being a famous athlete, a doctor or a fireman, a ballerina or a singer. Child prodigies often speak of such dreams. Your Vision is a personal fable, a story you tell to yourself about how you want to be in the future. A statement about possibilities and potential, it looks beyond the limitations of the present.

Thinking successfully demands that you have a goal on which to focus your attention. If you fasten your attention on what you already know, then you will only repeat the present in the future, albeit in some different form. Albert Schweitzer had achieved recognition as a university lecturer and a performer of Bach's organ music before he developed his vision of a healing mission. This took him beyond the comfortable confines of Alsace to Africa and his missionary life for which he became known worldwide. Your Vision creates a doorway into a different future, it begins to chart a path forward. Vision is your first step towards change.

A personal vision is your map to the future. As children we are given rules and guidelines on how to lead our lives. As adults our choices become less clearly defined. We have to begin to choose for ourselves – but making those decisions is often complicated by the endless considerations which seem to form the content of our daily lives. A personal vision helps you to choose a path through the infinite possibilities of life. It helps you find your way around obstacles, cuts through the undergrowth of life, and provides trail-marks and signposts to keep you on track. A personal vision is your guide to the future.

A Vision encompasses more than the routine details of life. It is something to which you return regularly for inspiration. When you seem lost on a sea of daily responsibilities or in some vast undergrowth of soulless administration, reconnecting with your Vision will reconnect you with the meaning and purpose of your life.

Your Vision is an inspiration. It helps make your life a work of art. Florence Nightingale once wrote, 'Being a nurse is an art; . . . after all, what's working with a blank canvas or a piece of cold marble compared with treating the human body – the temple of the divine spirit? It is one of the finest arts. I would even go so far as to say it is the finest of arts.'

Yet a Vision is more than an inspirational statement. It is a concrete and necessary start to an effective mental training programme. However idealistic your Vision may seem, it is actually the *foundation* of your systematic approach to mental training. If you don't take time to build it carefully and well, you will find the edifice of your plans crumbling at precisely the moment when it's most needed. Your Vision is the source of your plans, and although you may not know it yet, it is the source of your motivation to succeed. To understand fully the implications of this we need to explore the five attributes of a powerful Vision: **Potential**, **Purpose**, **Passion**, **Power**, and **Planning**.

Potential

A vision is a statement of your potential. When you create your Vision, you are imagining how things might be – how they could become. That said, you are not there yet. You may have the potential to be a great athlete or a brilliant actor but, unless you develop the physical, technical and mental skills required to transform it into form and action, you will never be more than a potential Carl Lewis, a potential John Gielguld or a potential Margaret Thatcher. The first step in actualising the potential you do have, is to create and energise your Vision of how you want to be.

Your Vision is rich with qualities that you want to bring into your life. Qualities are potential attributes of a person – often manifest to some degree, but seldom expressed fully. Typical qualities are: love, creativity, discrimination, discipline, consistency, joy, humour and power. We recognise these qualities in others, either in people we know or in the images of people we watch on film or television or about whom we read. Some images are so clear that the person portrayed appears to be the universal embodiment of a specific quality. Mother Theresa is the touchstone for service, John Cleese for humour, Henry Ford for industry, Picasso for creativity and Margaret Thatcher for power.

None of us have access to the full range of human qualities, and yet none of us are totally bereft of any of them. Your Vision is an acknowledgement of your own unique potential and as such, it should carry all those positive qualities that you identify as an integral part of its perfect expression. Whatever your potential may be, an effective mental training programme is essential if it is to be achieved. Formulating your Vision is the first step in this process.

Something almost unexpected happens as you achieve your potential: you begin to feel good about yourself. There is no other way to put it. There is a sense of satisfaction which accompanies the successful expression and use of your full ability. Cesar Chavex, who helped initiate a transformation in the treatment and civil rights of Hispanic labourers in America, commented on his observation of this process in his fellow workers:

One of the most beautiful and satisfying results of our work in setting up a workers' union in the fields is to see one of these workers developing an expression of the natural dignity which starts to shine out of a man when his worth is recognised. Even the employers notice it. Workers who until a short while ago had been treated as slow-witted members of a forgotten community suddenly blossom as they become able, intelligent people, imbued with initiative and the ability to lead others.

However the sense of satisfaction is not derived from the object you may have created: most artists soon move on to their next painting; a successful encounter in a tennis knock-out competition simply creates the opportunity to compete in the next round; a business deal closed frees you to move on to the next one. It's not the result which creates the sense of pleasure. Rather it's how, in creating the result, you have developed certain personal qualities. The object or result reflects some intangible but real aspect of you and what you are. Your potential has been 'actualised' – but you've still got the same or even more potential to move onwards!

If you were to compose a Vision statement for yourself now, how would it sound? You can't afford to be too easily satisfied. Your Vision statement, and indeed any expression of your Vision, has to be rich and evocative enough to provide an inspiration and guide to your inner self and to what you want to become. If the expression of your Vision does not evoke your full potential, you need to re-examine it. Pierre Rodin, the French sculptor, said:

As far as my work with models is concerned, I do not only need to have complete *knowledge* of the human form, I also need a feeling for every aspect of it. I must, so to speak, *embody* the lines of the human body and they must become part of me, deeply integrated into my instincts. I must become permeated by all the areas which it presents to the eye. I must feel it at my finger tips.

A Vision draws all parts of you into its expression and fulfillment. If your life doesn't offer you the opportunity to express and embody some of this potential you should ask yourself 'Why not?' And if you come to the conclusion that the direction you are heading in doesn't take you towards your potential, find out what keeps you from changing and whether you are willing to take the risks involved in change.

Purpose

A Vision has purpose. Purpose is an active principle. It is a force which moves you in the direction of a goal or objective. A Vision has purpose because it carries this desire to express, to achieve, to become something which may, as of yet, only be potential. When you have a purpose you can connect with some deeper, more central part of yourself. It's as if your Vision is your reason for being alive. It gives you the licence to express yourself in the world and the impetus to overcome obstacles on your path.

Purpose gives meaning to your every move, to life itself. Dag Hammarskjold, Secretary General of the United Nations from 1953 to 1961 wrote in his biography, *Markings*:

> I have inherited the conviction that no one life is more satisfying than one dedicated to the disinterested service of one's country – or of humanity. This service requires the sacrifice of all personal interests, but it also calls for the courage to fight resolutely for one's convictions about what is right and good for the community, whatever opinions might be fashionable at the time.

We all pursue a wide range of day-to-day activities. Some are challenging, some are easy, some take a long time, others a few seconds, some we enjoy and some we hate. And yet throughout them all should run a thread of purpose and meaning. 'I push myself through the last round of circuit training, because I know it will prepare me for Saturday's match.' 'I wade through this endless paperwork because I know it will ensure the financial go-ahead for my project.' 'I re-edit the last chapter of my book for the tenth time because only then will it express what I have to say.' In the above situations, you push yourself through barriers of physical pain or mental exhaustion because beyond it there is a purpose that gives meaning to what might otherwise be trivial action.

A purposeful Vision does something else. It gives order to your life. Purpose is a synthesising force. It creates a relationship between all your life's activities. It also acts as a prioritising principle. When you are in touch with the purpose in your Vision you can choose, from amongst the many opportunities in your life, those activities which will further your purpose and bring you closer to expressing your potential. Your Vision can help you see your life in a new and different way. You may find that what was formerly important no longer dominates, or the connection between hitherto unrelated areas suddenly becomes clear and strong. A Vision with purpose helps you make hard choices and clear decisions.

This purpose shouldn't be confused with blind determination. Being purposeful does not mean bulldozing your way through obstacles, even though you may sometimes need to do that. It doesn't mean running roughshod over people either, although if you are a team leader you may have to be firm in your decisions. Purpose is not just good old fashioned will-power, even though sometimes you may need to use strong will. Clarity of purpose can give meaning and order not just to your own life but to the lives of people around you as well.

This is particularly the case when your Vision includes the well-being of others. Such a Vision not only helps to get all the factors and actions in your life in the proper order, but also helps you get into a correct relationship with the people with whom you live and work. Mother Theresa of Calcutta said,

> Be kind. Do not let anyone leave you without being a better or happier person. Be a living expression of the kindness of God; kindness in your face, kindness in your eyes, kindness in your smile, kindness in your warm greeting.

Passion

You should hold your Vision passionately. Your Vision will be a distillation of your personal philosophy and reflect the ideals and values that give meaning to your life. A Vision that has purpose will help you to organise the activities of your life into an intelligible pattern. But a passionately held belief gives you the power to make that Vision work. It carries you and those around you, forward.

A Vision has the potential to create change and it is the passion of your Vision that powers that change. This passion generates the internal resources you require to redirect the course of your life away from habits and patterns of inertia and on to the path toward 'self-actualisation'. Paul Gauguin said about his inspiration as a painter:

> Where does the creation of a painting begin and end? When intense feelings are born deep within a person and ideas burst forth like lava from a volcano, is this not the appearance of an unexpectedly created work, brutal if you like, but certainly great and having a superhuman aspect?

A passionate Vision carries with it conviction and commitment. This is important because when you communicate your Vision to other people – friends, colleagues, customers, superiors – they will need to feel your passion. They won't ask you outright, 'Are you passionate about this idea of yours?' They may not even have formulated the question. Yet they will sense whether or not you are committed, whether or not you have the courage of your convictions. And in the final analysis it is this factor which tips the balance in favour of you getting the job, making the side, playing in an orchestra or winning the competition.

Piero Ferrucci, in his marvellous book *Inevitable Grace*, describes how contagious was the passion of the painter, Claude Monet:

> Monet, irritated by the criticisms that the mists he painted were not suitable subjects for a picture, responded by painting the smoke from a train. He set up his easel 'like a tyrant' (according to Renoir's son) at Saint Lazare station and, though not yet a well known artist, convinced the astonished station master of the Western Rail company to stop the trains at his request, get them to burn extra coal so they would produce more smoke, and change the timetable so he could catch the sunlight on the billowing steam: 'It is an enchantment, a true fantasmagorie', he told Renoir, 'who would ever have guessed that train smoke and a dirty station would generate a masterpiece.

Half-heartedness will not do! Check out just how passionately you hold your beliefs. Is your Vision a source of inspiration for you? If not, find out what fires the furnace of your enthusiasm and build it into your Vision. If your Vision doesn't capture your own imagination, if it isn't alive for you, you'll never mobilise the internal resources to express it, let alone attract the people, time, money and materials you need. Check that you're passionate about your Vision in private as well as public. If you're not you must go back to the drawing-board.

If there was a sports prize for passion in the 1980s it might well be won by Dennis O'Connor, the skipper of the American entry in the Americas Cup Races. Though not always liked (in part because his passion borders on obsession) he is widely respected. The first dramatic bout between O'Connor's American yacht and John Bertrand's Australia II was a riveting dance on the endlessly changing surface of the sea with the strenuous, abrupt, almost superhuman efforts of the crews displayed as a gracious sarabande on television screens across the world. In the end innovation (another product of Vision) won out against passion. Australia captured the cup, it was unbolted from the display stand at the New York Yacht Club and for the first time ever, was displayed in a foreign country where it was held hostage for the next three years. Yet O'Connor with his passionate Vision, refused to abandon the challenge. Eventually he managed to pull together a new American team, this time from the San Diego Yacht Club. After months of intensive trials and training, guided by O'Connor's Vision of excellence, the team left for Perth, Australia, where O'Connor's fierce passion carried them through into the final of the next Americas Cup Challenge. In the end, it was his passion too which inspired the team to overhaul the New Zealanders and to recapture the Cup, thereby vindicating his commitment to excellence. Tom Peters, American business guru, calls this passion 'bone-felt beliefs'.

Passion has immense power because it lifts your Vision beyond thoughts to something you feel and sense. There is an expression 'I want it so bad, I can almost taste it'. A passionate Vision has an image, a taste, a sound, a colour. You can have a symbol for it, a tune or a song. These all contribute to bringing your Vision to life. The more you can see it, hear it, feel it and – yes – even taste it, the more you will be able to move it from the level of potential to the world of reality.

Power

A Vision carries personal power. Your Vision is the vehicle for your dreams and aspirations. It is a source of motivation and inspiration. It acts as a compass when you are unsure as to the course of action you want to take. It captures your imagination and gives you the momentum to push through internal and external barriers.

The power of your Vision lies in recognising that it is yours. You have created it and it reflects your inner reality. Personal power is the product of your knowing and accepting who you are. When you produce your Vision you are actually taking hold of your hidden potential. This is very important since most of us deny or disown a greater or lesser part of who we really are. The process of reclaiming the disowned parts of ourselves is incredibly empowering and is very much a part of this book.

It is a long process – one that lasts for the rest of your life – but great success is the product of many small victories. This book is designed to help you to map out a systematic strategy whereby you may achieve your goals, express your potential and embody your Vision. You have phenomenal power when you align your daily actions with your potential and then direct them passionately towards your purpose.

A personal Vision, when implemented through a systematic action plan, acts like a magnifying glass on a sunny day. Perhaps as a child you played with a magnifying glass and discovered its ability to focus the rays of the sun on to a leaf or a piece of paper, which would begin to turn brown, smoke and eventually burst into flame. Your Vision focuses your potential. It collects the diffuse elements of your personality and organises them around goals and aspirations. It helps clarify your potential, drawing fantasies and dreams into those areas demanding your energy and self expression. Your Vision contains the disparate elements of your personality, ensuring they don't spill out into self-defeating confusion. It acts as a channel, aligning these elements deliberately to your purpose. This power is the power of your Vision.

Newton, when writing about how he discovered the law of universal gravitation said:

> By thinking about it continually I keep the object of my research constantly before me, waiting for the first light of understanding to emerge little by little; eventually the situation changes until the light is complete.

Your Vision provides the focus, the channel for the power of your mind, body and emotions.

Power gives you the ability to create change. At the simplest level, to move now from your chair to a window across the room, you need and use some of your power. In all activities of your life you use your personal power. Yet some people seem to have unlimited personal power. Their motivation not only moves themselves but often other individuals, teams and departments as well. Some have enough personal power to transform a whole organisation. Jan Carlzon, President and Chief Executive of Scandinavian Airline Systems has used such power in this way.

Martha Graham transformed the world of modern dance through her Vision which motivated her entire dance company to embody and carry it into the world. This same power enabled Graham to dance until she was over 60 years old.

The expression of personal power is encountered throughout society. A colleague of ours who played in a brass band described the difference between one bandmaster and another. With the first, a chord could be a disparate collection of notes, from a group of individuals with little in common with one another. With the second, the chord would rise to the ceiling and wind its way through the consciousness of each and every member of the band. By focusing his personal power on the production of a single chord, the second bandmaster had achieved total musical and interpersonal harmony.

In these and many other cases the power of the individual is the product of an ability to focus all personal resources on the task whilst creating a meaningful context for action and the actions of others. In other words the individual has a Vision of how things are to be, focused all personal resources on that Vision and successfully put into place a plan for it to be implemented.

Planning

Planning is your strategy for encapsulating your Vision. It was Louis Pasteur who said: 'Chance only favours the prepared mind.' Visions don't automatically become reality. We know of no secret formula which will change pumpkins into carriages or wishes into success at the snap of your fingers. You will need to spend time planning and implementing your course of action. You will need to take a close look at yourself and evaluate your strengths and weaknesses. You'll need to mobilise your resources both internal and external, to support you in pursuit of your goals. Indeed, you'll have to allocate time to develop your Vision, set your goals and take the steps or practice the exercises which will allow you to achieve those goals. All this takes planning.

It may come as a surprise to learn that neither Visions nor plans are rigid. They change. As you grow they grow. As you change they change. You may feel that, having developed a Vision and organised a good plan of action you have only to follow the plan systematically to realise your Vision. That's not enough! Your plan will change from month to month, from day to day, sometimes from moment to moment.

Revising your course of action is like tending a garden – each time you return to it you assess whether you have positioned everything correctly – enjoying those parts of the plan that are in right proportion and producing fruit, tending those parts that are neglected, changing or moving those parts that are suffering, cutting back those that are too dominant and making more room for those plans which you want to foster and encourage. The process never ends.

When you plan how you will implement your Vision, you are making a long-term commitment to yourself. As long as it remains a Vision, it stays on the level of potential. It is only what might happen. When you plan you demonstrate good faith. When you begin to act on your plan, you are keeping your agreement by demonstrating your commitment to fulfill your potential and achieve your purpose.

Your plan and the pursuit of it has one more attribute. This is the way in which you begin consciously to move from the present to the future. This role of consciously creating change in yourself is crucial. When you choose change and plan how to move forward, you step out of the situation, distancing or 'disidentifying' yourself from the old you and from your old limitations, habits, patterns and weaknesses. You become an agent for change rather than the problem which needs changing. This allows you to assume a new role and identity beyond the confines of your past experience or future expectations.

Habitual patterns of thought and action close down possibilities for new experience and achievement. Habitual thinking will eventually immobilise an individual just as it will immobilise a large organisation. Chris Evert prolonged an immensely successful career by taking a decision to begin to attack the net. From a confirmed backcourt player she suddenly became a net player and eventually an all-rounder. This change re-energised her tennis, confounded her opponents and probably improved her enjoyment of tennis as well. She became her own agent of change.

Kate also became an agent for change. Stuck in her large house with two small children, she still felt unfulfilled. But every time she made a move, the demands of running the house and looking after the children became too much. What she really wanted to do was to retrain and go out to meet people, but it was always easier to stay at home. Eventually, she wrote down her aims, and planned her strategy, with a clarity of purpose and passion that helped her cater for the other demands. Two years on, she wonders how she lasted so long doing the same thing. Lack of perspective is probably one of the most effective of jailors.

By becoming your agent for change you develop the ability to maintain a dual perspective on your own performance. On one day you might be in a situation which requires instant action, on another, you can step out of the problem, become your own coach and objective observer, thereby assuring that you aren't stuck or becoming the problem yourself.

The author, pilot and war correspondent, Antoine de Saint Exupéry captures the transcendent experience of full self-actualisation:

> Suddenly, by virtue of a midnight experience which has stripped you of everything that is superfluous, you discover in yourself a person you did not know was there . . . Someone great whom you will never forget. And this is you . . . This person has spread his wings, he is no longer attached to the transient benefits of this world, he has accepted the possibility of dying for all men and has thus entered into something universal. A strong sigh comes from his lips. There he is, exposed, the sovereign lord who lay sleeping within you: man. You are on a par with the music in his composition, and with the physicist who pushes back the frontiers of knowledge . . . you have reached that height where all loves have a common measure. Perhaps you have suffered, maybe you have felt alone, your body may have found no place of refuge, but in those open arms today you have been received by love.

Creating your Vision is the first step in becoming who you truly are.

2

Getting your personal Vision

Visioning the future

Visionaries are the folk heroes of our modern age. These are
the people who see how the future will be before it happens
and thereby influence that future. Billie Jean King, the one
individual most responsible for bringing women's tennis out
of the shadow of the men's game and into a world class
professional circuit was able to visualise what the future world
of women's professional tennis would look like. Whilst male-
dominated officialdom and many journalists made disparaging
comments she focused her attention on her Vision of how
things would be.

Steven Jobs represents another such visionary. In 1975,
with Steve Woznik, he founded Apple computers. Their
goal of transforming computers into user-friendly instruments
accessible to people in all walks of life was first viewed with
disdain. Then, as the market implications became apparent,
IBM, Compaq, Olivetti, NEC, Toshiba and a string of lesser
manufacturers scrambled to climb aboard the user-friendly
bandwagon.

Clive Sinclair of Sinclair Computers – also a visionary –
believed that computers should not only be user-friendly but
also affordable. His range of inexpensive, compact personal
computers priced at under £100 found a large market in the

UK where the per capita ownership of personal computers became larger than the much touted PC market in the USA. Alan Sugar's Amstrad built on this demand for affordable computers and his Amstrad range met the demand of higher powered computers which cost hundreds rather than thousands of pounds. In the course of two years Amstrad shares increased over 1000% in value on the stock market.

These men envisioned a future in which computers were easy to work with and affordable to the general public at a time when computers were still clumsy and complex machines requiring huge outlays of money and highly trained staff to operate them. They had the vision to see what the future held before it happened.

A future thinker sees the present in the context of the future. It's now time to guide you to discovering your own personal vision – but only if you are prepared to be an innovator. You have to decide in advance whether you are willing to re-create your present life so that it fulfills your Vision – whatever that may turn out to be. This means reassessing your assumptions about who you are and where you are heading in your life and then thinking about the future without the constraints of the past. In 1983, Harvard Business School professor, Rosabeth Moss Kanter, defined such future thinkers as 'change masters'. We are asking you to become a 'change master' in your own life, to take part in the process of change.

Making a start

Begin by getting yourself an A4 hardback exercise book. This will be the first volume of your log-book. You will be writing in it at each step along the way, as you compose and carry out your mental training programme.

We begin with some exercises designed to help you get a vision of the future you want to create. These allow you consciously to direct your ability to fantasise about the future. They are excursions into your potential – just as you might make an excursion to the Arctic Circle or the Far East. To make this first journey you need a comfortable chair, your book and pen in hand, and to be undisturbed for up to 30 minutes.

Sit back, relax and let your mind wander. Think about your past. What was it like? What were your goals and ambitions when you were growing up? What did you want to do, to become? How have you organised your life in the past? What did you study? Where did you train? Who did you work with? Who were key individuals in your life? What were the momentous events in your life: Perhaps your first job? Getting married? Buying a home? Promotion? Winning an important competition? Playing a Bach sonata? Take about five minutes to let your thoughts range over your past life, without staying in any one place or time. Then stop.

Take a moment to let go of your thoughts about the past, then bring your attention to the present. Begin now to reflect on your present life. How do you spend most of your time? What are your major concerns? What is the state of your work? Your home? Your family? What are the major initiatives in your life? At what do you most want to succeed? How much of your time do you spend on mental preoccupation? Emotional concerns and relationships? Physical training, exercise, performance? How do you relax? What are your major pursuits outside of your career? Take five to ten minutes to review your present life, simply sitting and reflecting on the way it is. Stay in the present, but don't stick to one event or area of your life. Then stop.

Then allow your thoughts about the present to fade. Sit back, relax and close your eyes. Imagine that you are going into the future, and you are visiting a land of the future where you will live one day. This land is the product of your efforts. It is your Visionary land. It embodies all that you have dreamed about. It also embodies many ideas that you have never even considered. Possibilities that are new, maybe even startling, will present themselves to you. Allow that to happen. Spend some time and see what this future land is like and what you will have created. What kind of friends, colleagues, team mates have you attracted to yourself? Have you built a business? Written books? Have you helped other people? Is there a family in this future? What courses, training, experiences have you been through? What skills have you acquired? What have you invented, built and developed? Where have you performed, worked and visited?

As you travel through this imaginary land of the future, open your eyes, take your pen and paper and jot down what you see. You may want to close your eyes again to get more images and then open them to write. You may prefer to keep your eyes open fantasising and writing alternately. Do whatever works best. If you repeat yourself, that's okay. Remember this is just an excursion. You have probably fantasised many times before about your future. This is simply an opportunity to do so now with permission in a systematic way.

Take as long as you need to fantasise about the future. When you have finished your excursion and writing, go back over what you have written. Take a red pen or pencil and underline or circle those thoughts, ideas, situations and accomplishments that are the most powerful or striking. It may be everything or just a few key events, mark whatever is especially significant to you. As you read through what you have written, new ideas may come to you. Write them down as well. When you've completed this you've finished the first stage of visioning your future.

Let's pause here and ask how you did. Turn the page of your log book and describe in a few sentences how you felt. Did you enjoy fantasising or not? Was it hard or was it easy? Was it strange or familiar? Maybe you were told not to daydream when you were a child at school and found the exercise made you feel guilty or impatient? If so, let us remind you again that great achievers – such as you may now aspire to be – have always been different.

All visionaries dream a great deal. They spend time thinking about things considered little by other people. Sometimes they are accused of living in a world of unreality . . . Until they make it real. We only asked you to drop your guard against fantasising, to let down your intellectual guard long enough to explore your future potential. The German poet, Friedrich von Schiller once said:

> It would seem that it is not a helpful thing, and indeed it can be counterproductive to the creative work of the spirit, if the intellect is used too rigorously to examine ideas as they arrive at the threshold of the mind. Considered by itself, an idea may be completely insignificant and unworkable; but it could become important in light of a subsequent idea; perhaps when combined with other equally insignificant ideas it could form part of a functioning whole . . . In a creative mind . . . I would say that the intellect has withdrawn its guards from the gates so that ideas can burst in at random and only then the intellect examines them altogether.

If you still find this hard to take and can't help responding 'but Schiller was only a poet. I have to operate in the real world', consider that hard-headed business man Conrad Hilton. Long before there were hotel chains like Trusthouse Forte, Ramada, Holiday Inn, Great Western and so forth, Hilton dreamed of a hotel chain that spread around the world and which offered a uniform standard of service. At the time it seemed far-fetched but Hilton saw a future in which people would constantly travel around the world, stopping in one major city after another. He saw they would require easy checking in and out, assured forward booking, quality service and consistent standards. The Hilton chain grew out of that vision. To us today it is unremarkable. In its time it was the stuff of dreams.

The truth is that *your* Vision can be your inspiration, it can organise your personal experience, goals and objectives. And the first step is to harness your ability to fantasise about the future.

Visioning how you will be in the future

The next step is to embody yourself clearly within your Vision. It's not enough to know how you want to be. You also need to be able to feel and experience being that way with all of your senses: seeing, hearing, feeling, even conjuring up the sensations of taste and smell.

Review what you wrote about your future world in the previous exercise. Read it through carefully and calmly and then set it aside, sit back, close your eyes, slowly allow yourself to relax undisturbed for up to 15 minutes.

Now, in your mind's eye, revisit your land of the future. Imagine that you are on a hill, looking down into a valley which is this land. Begin to walk down into this valley, noticing as before what this world is like, what is happening, who is there and what they are doing. As you arrive at the centre of the valley, perhaps the town square, you see someone standing there, surveying the scene.

As you approach, you realise that this is the future you. You move forward, approach the future you and then step inside. *Become* this person. Take a moment to become aware of how you feel being this way . . .

Then begin to walk around and visit your future world. As you come to each different area – home, work, sport, colleagues, friends, ideas, books, articles, hobbies – observe carefully and notice what *in you* contributed to or created that valuable part of your future. Was it perseverance that took you through that degree programme? Was it creativity that developed your team? Was it perhaps humour that joined your family together? Was it spontaneity, reliability or courage that helped your sporting performance? Was it calm reflection that laid the foundation for your book? What is it that you carry in yourself that was the seed for your future creations? What qualities do you embody that make possible the achievement of your goals? How did you grow and develop in your skills and experiences to be able to produce what you have done?

As you conduct this tour, be particularly aware of how you feel as you connect with each of your inner qualities which are at the core of the different things and experiences of your future world. How do you feel when you are determined? How do you act when you feel spontaneous? What thoughts accompany your burst of creativity? Savour each quality, connecting with the feelings, thoughts and sensations you experience as you embody the future you . . .

Finish the tour and take a few moments to reflect, making notes in your log book. What are the key qualities, activities, ideas, approaches that characterise you in this future land of yours? If the first exercise – your first visit to this land – was about the *what* of your future, this exercise is more about the *how*. How do you embody those attributes that you found you needed to achieve your ideas and dreams? How does it feel? As you write, think about those qualities, attributes and skills that you are going to develop in order to make your Vision a reality. How will you become the individual you visualised and experienced in your excursion?

You are being asked to go deeper this time, to discover not only what the world around you will look like but also how you want to be in this future world. It is these personal attributes which will make or break your strategies and goals. If you've got them or can learn to develop them, you will be successful in achieving your goals. Include the cultivation of these qualities and attributes in your plans as well: note what you don't yet possess, and work out how you can get it.

Personal qualities such as passion, commitment, discipline, creativity, enthusiasm, joy, perseverance and will are vital to the success of your Vision. Psychologists identify certain drives – aggression, territorality, survival, the need for security, nurturing one's young, sexual drive – as part of our biological make-up. As animals we inherit these drives. However, the personal qualities that are such an important part of your Vision are essentially human. They are just as much a part of your essential nature as your animal instincts. By embodying them you begin to express your potential and it is precisely your ability to connect with this potential which brings you and your Vision to life.

Expressing your Vision

You are now ready to produce a Vision statement. This statement will create the context for your future goals. A Vision statement looks to the future. It defines how you will be, what you want to become, how you will grow and develop. Your Vision statement is a guide for future decisions.

Turn back the pages of your log book and reread what you wrote during the last two exercises: the account of your future world, and the description of how you will be and what qualities you will embody when you are part of that world. As you read, reconnect with the thoughts, experiences and feelings associated with these two excursions. Note down on a fresh page or underline the key ideas, aspirations and qualities which you feel should be included in your Vision statement. Reflect on them and, when you are ready, begin to compose your statement. Here are some guidelines to help you write it:

- Keep it simple. Make your sentences and paragraphs concise and to the point.

- It should all fit on one page of your log-book so that you can view the whole statement at once.

- Keep out dates, time frames, measurements and numbers.

- Make the statement challenging. This is a call to action so it should evoke the best you have to offer and provide a fitting goal to which you can aspire.

- Make sure the statement increases your sense of personal power. It should be empowering for you specifically.

- Although you are aspiring to the future, include and affirm the best from the past.

- Be specific about qualities, aspirations and attributes. Name them in your Vision statement.

- Write in the present and future tense, using the first person singular. For instance, 'I will be professional in my approach to my clients. As I grow more professional, I express my enthusiasm and interest in their needs.'

- Make sure your Vision statement is one you can demonstrate in your daily life. You should be able to bring the statement to life.

It may take you several sittings to polish your Vision statement. You have to discover how to include all the elements you want, whilst keeping it clear and succinct. The statement should have some internal coherence. Don't try to include everything and anything. Tune in to your Vision and allow the major themes to emerge.

You may decide to set your statement aside for a few days before returning to refine it. Take the time you need but be aware that there is some urgency. You are developing your Vision statement for immediate use. So keep in touch with your task. Carry your Vision with you every day.

When you have composed your Vision statement (and have had time to admire it), develop a personal slogan. Read through your Vision statement or sit back and tune in to the Vision itself and see what emerges – some simple phrase which captures it all. Slogans are seldom more than a dozen words, often less.

If you want a slogan and can't pull out of the air an all-encompassing phrase, you could begin by adopting one sentence from your Vision statement or summarising several elements. However don't try to squeeze too much into it, make it one clear primary concept.

Another way to keep your Vision with you from day to day
is to find a melody or tune that evokes it for you in a way that
words alone cannot. When you read your statement and tune
in to your Vision, reflect on the kind of music that embodies
its passion or theme. Music may touch both your emotions and
mind. It can reach your 'bone-deep beliefs'. So, if it suits you,
find a musical theme for your Vision as a film director does for
his film.

Packaging

When you have captured your Vision statement, take some
time to write or print it out. Put it on a card and set it on
your desk. Get a calligrapher to write it out for you and have
it framed. Reduce it on a photocopying machine so that you
can carry it on a card or used it for a book mark in your diary.
And, of course, write it prominently on the inside cover of your
log-book.

Don't forget to use the slogan too. Put it at the top of your
Vision statement. If appropriate, include it on your stationery.
Use it as a theme for talks, presentations, or articles you may
write. Flaunt it! No-one else will!

Change as a constant

Having tuned into your potential, grounding it in a solid,
inspiring and meaningful Vision, you have the direction and
context you need to set goals and develop the action steps
necessary for achieving those goals. Your Vision will be the
cornerstone of your personal growth for the next period of
time.

However, everything changes. Your personal Vision is the
most relevant, up-to-date and appropriate Vision that exists
for you *at this time*. In a year it may still be so . . . but aspects of
it will change. As you grow and develop, and begin to embody
your Vision, you will discover things about yourself that you
don't know at the moment. New goals and aspirations will

emerge. Further horizons may present themselves. Be alert for new possibilities. Be open to them they arise. Meantime, the best way to create new opportunities in the future is to get on with putting your Vision into action now.

3

Grounding your Vision

Having realised the need to take stock and having granted yourself the time to get the big picture, the next stage is to ground your Vision by setting goals. This is the final stage of the Visioning process. True goalsetting still involves looking to the ideal, aspiring to your potential and using your imagination. At this stage, though, you will need to make a further commitment to yourself to turn the dreams and fantasies of your Vision into concrete goals and objectives. The goals you are about to set will act as the bridge between your Vision and the strategies and tactics you'll devise to actualise your Vision.

Goalsetting involves the use of the analytical side of your brain. Until now you've been 'thinking of' your future, now is the time to 'think about' it. If the Visioning process has been non-linear, associative and full of images, the goal-setting process involves making lists, verbalising the abstract ideas of your Vision and making the components of your Vision discrete, specific and tangible. However creative and intuitive you are, if you want to make your dreams come true, you need to reflect pragmatically and set realistic goals.

The goal-setting exercise

You will need:

- your Vision statement

- your description of your ideal self

- your description of your ideal 'land'

- your log-book, a red and a black pen

- about 60 minutes

Take five to ten minutes to reread the visioning you've done so far: look over the notes you took on your ideal land and your ideal self, and reconsider your Vision statement. Then sit back and reflect. Perhaps you'd like to play the melody or theme song that goes with your Vision as you do so. Allow your thoughts to range widely over the Vision of your future.

When you are ready, take out your log-book and at the top of a new page write: **Lifetime Goals**. Give yourself five to ten minutes to write down *all* your lifetime goals, particularly those inspired by your Vision. Take all the time you need to make your list complete. What position do you want to achieve at work? How big do you want your company to grow? What income do you want to attain? What competition do you want to take part in? What competitions do you want to win? What skills do you want to perfect? What diplomas, degrees or qualifications do you want to gain? What books, articles or stories do you want to write? What companies do you want to work with? What would you like to perform? What kind of family do you want? Where do you want to live? Where do you want to travel?

Write down each goal in a way that reflects your Vision. It may be that you want to focus specifically on your Vision as it relates to your sport, your career or your relationships. That's fine. Just be clear when you begin that you are focusing on a specific, albeit important area in you life. Make certain however that your goals are still in line with your Vision.

Your list should have at least a dozen goals. Twenty or thirty is not too many. When you have completed the list to your satisfaction, stop. Turn over the page and don't look back for the present.

At the top of the page write: **Five-year Goals**. Again, make a list. This time, take five to ten minutes to write down all the goals you want to achieve in the next five years. Make, the list as comprehensive as the one you've just done. When you have taken all the time you need – no less than five minutes – put down your pen. Turn the page and don't look back at it for the present.

At the top of the next page write: **One-year Goals**. As before, take ten minutes to make a comprehensive list, before turning that page over.

Finally, at the top of the next page write: **One-month Goals**. Complete this page as you have the previous three, taking at least five minutes – and listing a minimum of 12 goals – 20 to 30 being even better, if you can. If you get stuck, refer back to your Vision – the statement and the descriptions of your future land and ideal self. Let them spark off additional ideas, goals and aspirations, regardless of how big or small they may be. Take all the extra time you need. Be as specific as you like.

When you have completed this list, draw a line beneath it. By interpreting your Vision in terms of goals and having introduced a time-frame, you have already taken the first step towards the future you have identified and chosen.

Setting Priorities

The next step is to look back through your four lists of objectives and decide which in each list are the most important. Too often we spend far too long and far too much energy on attaining objectives which:

- are not really important to us

- don't reflect our true aspirations

- give too little return on the effort put into them

- are things we think we should do because someone else said we should do them

- are actually contrary to our own best interests

You now need to give your goals 'A' 'B' and 'C' priorities.

An 'A' priority is one that is both *urgent* and *important* (prompting growth). Too often goals are prioritised on the basis of first come first served: whatever lands on your desk gets your immediate attention; whatever you are doing continues to occupy your time. Important priorities are often ignored because they involve difficult decisions or a commitment of time and energy that seems daunting. This is the wrong way to prioritise and often results in difficult but important matters being shunted to the bottom of the pile.

'Important' means that it is in line with your Vision and a significant contributor to you achieving your potential. 'A' priorities promote growth. They fulfil your potential, they move you out of old patterns into new ones, they complete unfinished business so you can move on without looking over your shoulder. If your goal isn't growth-orientated, why bother to pursue it?

'B' priorities can be as important as 'A' priorities but they are not so urgent. They can be as significant and growth orientated as your 'A' priorities only they can wait a while. When you give one of your goals a 'B' priority, you are saying, 'This is important and valuable to me. I want it to happen but the situation doesn't require immediate action.'

'C' priorities are those goals you want to happen but which are less important than your 'A' and 'B' priorities and also less urgent than the 'A's. They still need to be chosen because they help you grow towards your Vision. So you need to acknowledge their value. Keep them on your priority list and in your awareness as you evaluate the progress you make towards higher priority goals. 'C' priorities may be upgraded at any time.

The remaining goals are still important. However, they are not prioritised and you put them on hold, keeping them on your lists. Don't cross anything out. As you progress towards achieving your prioritised goals, some previously unranked goals may suddenly become important. Be prepared to review these goals regularly and see if their status changes.

To help you set priorities, and decide whether a goal is important, use the following guidelines.

- **You like the goal** Does this goal please you? Do you feel good about achieving it? Does it send tingles up and down your spine? This factor is so important! If you don't like the goal, however important it is, you will have great difficulty achieving it. It will be at best an arduous process. The experience of working towards goals is often more beneficial than the moment of achievement. If you don't enjoy the getting there, place this goal low on your priorities.

- **It brings alive some aspect of your Vision** Your goals are central to the strategies you will establish to make your Vision real. If there are no connections between the goal and your Vision, then re-examine why you want to pursue it. It's probably leading you down a false path.

- **It is connected to other goals** Is there some connection between it and your other goals? Most of us need to focus our efforts into specific directions. If goals and objectives have too wide a spread they may become increasingly difficult to achieve. Look for common threads.

- **You express your personal potential through achieving this goal** Goals should be more than just making things, building businesses or winning games. Achieving a goal should allow you to connect with some particular quality within yourself, to become more of who you really are. Many of your goals will be specific, making you focus on object-orientated activities. Don't let such goals dominate. Look for the promise of growth, self-actualisation and personal satisfaction in your goals.

- **Other people benefit**   This is important. If achieving this goal involves a team effort be sure that the whole team stands to gain. It should be a win/win situation. Ask yourself these questions: would a colleague, a supplier, or a loved one also gain when you achieve this goal? Does it offer a service? As you achieve this goal, will other people's quality of life somehow be improved? These and similar concerns are important because, when others benefit from our achievements, not only do you feel better but they also feel better and are inclined to help you in your efforts rather than hinder.

- **This goal helps build something bigger than you**   Do you create something? Does a business, a team, a product, a work of art, a book, grow out of this goal? Will you produce something on your own or in collaboration with others which you might not achieve otherwise?

- **You gain recognition**   Let's face it. We all like appreciation and recognition. Do you get some sense of acknowledgement or enhanced self-worth through pursuing this goal? If the pursuit of this goal brings out hidden potential, it is worthwhile.

- **It is unique, innovative, and creative**   Life should be more than hard, nose-to-the-grindstone work. There should be times of innovation, discovery and exploration. Make sure some of your goals are new. Moving into areas which are new to you provides growth and stimulation. Such goals will keep you young in mind and heart.

- **You are committed to making this goal happen** Are you *sure* you are really going to make the goal happen? Is it rather just a pipe dream, incidental to your deeper purpose and direction? If so, then reconsider the goal's priority. Don't throw it out. Just examine whether or not you really want it to happen. If you have some doubt, give it a lower priority.

- **It's fun** The fun element is essential. If goal-setting has slotted you back into a familiar rut of tension, unrealistic deadlines and boring accomplishments, leaving you no time for fun, joy or play, think again. It's time to lighten up!

Now take out your log-book and prioritise each of your four lists (lifetime, five-year, one-year and one-month). For each, allocate three 'A' priorities, three 'B' priorities and three 'C' priorities.

When you have finished, take a moment to sit back and congratulate yourself. You've cleared the decks, charted your course and launched yourself towards your Vision. You're ready to develop an action plan and begin taking concrete steps toward implementing your goals. But first you will need to examine your current situation, assessing your personal performance skills to see which may need improvement, what obstacles lie in your path and what resources you have to overcome them. It's time to assess where you are now!

4

Where are you now?

Having decided where you want to go, it is time to look at where you are now, what obstacles there are to your progress and what resources you have available to help you on your way.

Skills assessment

In this exercise you will have to step off the treadmill of your daily routine and take on the role of the interested observer. It is an exercise we first developed and still use with all sports clients, whether working with them as individuals or as members of a team. However, over the past few years, as we've charted a parallel course into the business world, we've used it successfully with business clients as well. Whether you want to forge new relationships, sail around the world on your own or paint like Picasso – this exercise gives you the opportunity to take stock of your current ability and get clear where you must next focus your attention. This is an essential part of thinking to win.

This is an analytical exercise that involves thinking *about* your performance. Its first benefit is that it makes you aware how many different skills are involved. Immediately, you learn that it is both simplistic and detrimental to your performance to say you had a good day and are doing well or had a bad day and are doing badly, without further comment. This is an example (though admittedly a common one) of lazy thinking, of how **not** to think. On the other hand, if you're specific but focus only on some horrendous gaffe you made with a client over lunch, the likelihood is that you'll make a similar mistake within the next few days. Okay, so you were thinking about something else at the time. Perhaps your listening skills are below par and need attention. What about all the other skills involved in meeting a client? At which of these did you actually excel?

As we found with athletes, the exercise gives a balanced outlook. If you are inclined to dwell on your mistakes it will encourage you, whereas if you are an incurable optimist or a self-satisfied superstar it will help you to be more realistic and stir yourself to further efforts to learn. The fact of the matter is that few people are used to thinking purposefully either *about* or *of* their performance. One is far more likely to consider someone else's performance in this way than one is to consider one's own.

When we are invited by a sports body to speak about mental training, or even when we are asked to lead a longer course, the participants (who are nearly always coaches) come armed with pens and paper for information *about* what we do, with the half-formulated expectation that they will then be able to go back to their teams and do at least a large part of what we do. Such expectations are rooted in the culture of our educational system. At an early age we are told to take notes on what is said so that we can repeat it back at a later date to our examiner or, in the case of these coaches, to their athletes.

We don't believe this is very useful. We don't believe anyone can take in and *digest* information until they have had some direct experience of the principles involved. We therefore begin by providing that experience.

So when it comes to the **skills assessment exercise**, we hand out two sheets of paper. On one is listed the skills required of the athlete, the squash player if it is a course for squash coaches, the American football player if it is a course for American football coaches, and on the other is listed the skills required of the coach. We then ask each coach to assess his or her own personal performance – as a coach.

When we work with a department in a large organisation, the procedure is the same. The **skills assessment** exercise is still designed for the individual. If you were to call us in to improve the performance of your subordinates, we would ask you to assess your own performance as manager as well. The skills required of a manager are different to those required of subordinates but you are a key part of your departmental team. Your performance as manager determines to a great extent how well your team and the individuals within it perform. If you as manager were not to do the exercise you would be largely wasting your company's money and our time.

That is why we keep reiterating that this book is only for those readers who are prepared to step back and assess their own performance, no matter what that performance may entail. Admittedly one of the skills required of a team leader is to assess the ability and performance of the team members. That is why we hand out two sheets of paper to the coaches who come on our course. *After* the course, they can either xerox and hand out the 'players' sheet' to their athletes for them each to complete or they can fill in a simplified version which shows their own assessment of each athlete's performance of each skill. (Usually we suggest they do both.)

Whether or not your Vision relates to holding a position within a team, this book is designed to guide you to a similar direct and personal experience. So if you are ready to move on, let's take this time to discover where you are at – and work out where it is that you need to go.

In this exercise you identify what your level of skills are, what level of skills the task requires and what the disparity between you and the required skill levels are. Your backhand may be well developed but your concentration under pressure abysmal. You may have creative ideas to present in your sales pitch, but lack the self confidence to put them over. As a writer your proficiency in the language may be excellent but your ability to generate powerful imagery sorely lacking.

Take out your one-month and one-year goals to help you.

Turn to the next page in the log book and copy the form illustrated on page 46.

At the top of the sheet write your name, the title of your job (or your position in the area of life you are changing) and the date. For instance 'Patrick Webb, Manager, 29 December 1990' or 'Jane Stubbs, aspiring actress, 30 June 1990'.

Under physical skills, make a list of the physical skills you need for your job. We would, for example, ask all athletes and coaches, whatever their sport to write:

> strength
> speed
> stamina
> flexibility
> agility
> balance
> timing
> ability to relax
> ability to sleep
> nutrition

When making your list you might well include some examples or perhaps specific aspects of one or other of the skills listed, for example, under 'strength', upper body strength or lower body strength.

Now move to the next column and list the technical skills of your performance.

Technical skills vary both within a field, and obviously from field to field. For example, the technical skills of management will vary according to the position. Tony Lewis, Manager of Education and Training (Manufacturing) at Ford of Europe defined the technical skills of his job as:

PHYSICAL SKILLS	TECHNICAL SKILLS	MENTAL SKILLS

problem solving
communicating
   – internally
   – externally
negotiating
   – with peers
   – with subordinates
   – with other parts of the organisation
   – with those providing a service
delegating
coaching and counselling
prioritisation
synthesising data
resource management
   – of cash
   – of people
presentation
   – of self
   – of company
   – of ideas

Here are some technical skills typical of other areas:

Volleyball player	**Guitar player**
Serving	Finger dexterity
Service reception	Sight reading
Passing	Scales
Spiking	High notes
Blocking	Difficult chords
Field defence	Keeping time
	Listening
	Tuning

When working with sports people and even with people with other occupations we produce forms such as the one on page 47, with the physical and mental skills already listed, these being roughly the same for *any* performance, but leaving the technical skills column blank, as these vary from sport to sport and occupation to occupation. You may find it easier to list and order and subdivide your technical skills on an additional sheet of paper first and you may want to discuss your list with someone else who performs or works with you before finalising it.

Now for the final column, the list of mental skills you need, to greater or lesser degree, if you are to perform well. We suggest that you copy down the following list to begin with:

> concentration
> confidence
> motivation
> ability to deal with pressure
> qualities
>   – determination
>   – patience
>   – clarity
>   – courage
>   – ingenuity
>   – humour
>   – flexibility
> attitudes towards
>   – competitors or opponents
>   – colleagues or team mates
>   – environment
>   – oneself

You may want to add to this list, especially to the list of qualities of performance, but check that you're not duplicating something written in this column or in one of the other two columns first. Don't cross out any of this list unless you feel a 100 per cent sure that such a skill could never be of any use to you.

When you've finished, review the entire spectrum of skills and check that you haven't missed anything.

Now go back to the first list, the physical skills, and score yourself out of ten for your *present ability* at each skill in turn. Write these scores against each skill in the first of the three subcolumns. Then score your ability at each of the technical skills you have listed in the same way, putting the figure in the first subcolumn. Finally do the same with each mental skill. When you come to a heading with subcategories, just put a score against each subcategory, not against the main heading.

Then go back to the list of physical qualities and score each in turn out of ten for how *important* that skill is to your performance. So, if you are a teacher, you may score the importance of strength at 1, the importance of eating well as 6 and the importance of being able to relax as 8. Or, if you are a construction worker, you may score strength as 9 out of 10 important, flexibility as 4 out of 10 and the ability to sleep as 5 out of 10. Whatever scores you come up with, write them against the skills concerned in the *second* narrow column.

Do the same with your list of technical and mental skills.

The last step is to go back to the list of physical skills and subtract the figure in the first column from the figure in the second column. Put the answers in the third narrow column. Be careful as you do this because some of the figures you write in the third column will be minus figures – the score you gave for ability in the first column might be higher than the score you gave for importance. When you've done this, do the same with your lists of technical and mental skills.

Now let's see what you've come up with. What sort of picture has emerged? Look at the physical skill scores first. What is the highest positive figure in the third column? Notice which skill or skills it is against and underline those skills (don't underline the figure). So, if you look down the third narrow column and see that highest figure is 3 and that it occurs twice, – against 'stamina' and against 'food' – underline 'stamina' and 'food'. Do the same with the technical and mental skills.

Having done that, put an asterisk against the skill with the highest score *overall*. If two skills or more have the same score, decide which you want to improve first and put an asterisk against that one.

You now have a complete picture. This is how you rate your performance at the moment. Here is the full complexity of that performance, the areas that you consider to be strong and those that you feel need to be strengthened. When working with athletes we always suggest that they sit down with their coach or manager and review the form together. The manager may agree with the assessment (the more experienced the player, the more likely the manager is to agree), in which case the discussion moves on to what technical training the athlete can do to improve the high-scoring skills, beginning with the skill he has asterisked. Later, the athlete sits down with one of us and works out a programme of mental training exercises to improve those same skills.

However, it might be that the manager's assessment of the athlete varies with the athlete's own assessment. This does not invalidate the athlete's effort. By doing the exercise he has made himself conscious of his own self-image, which in turn affects or even determines how he performs. If the manager or coach tells him he thinks the player is *better* at some skills than the player is rating himself, then the player is likely to gain confidence in those areas and perform those skills still better. If on the other hand, the manager or coach says he thinks the player is rating himself too high at certain skills then he will turn his attention to what previously had been a blind spot for him.

In the 1988 BBC1 TV programme *QED: With a Goal in Mind*, which showed John Syer working with the London First Division football team, Queens Park Rangers, there is a shot of Peter Shreeve, the team coach, telling Martin Allen that he shouldn't be worrying too much about his lack of speed, that Martin was unnecessarily comparing himself with his team-mate Paul Parker who is one of the fastest players in the league. Instead Peter guided Martin's attention towards the technical skill of composure on the ball.

The result of the exercise, despite the discrepancy between Martin's view of his own performance and the coaching staff's view, was entirely positive. In the first place Martin, as all the other players in the team, had sat down for the first time and thought hard about the different components of his performance. Secondly, Martin discovered that he was not being judged adversely on his speed, that he was considered perfectly competent at this skill for his role on the pitch.

Thirdly, the coaching staff discovered that they hadn't made it clear to Martin what they required from him by way of improvement and subsequently gave him extra attention for a few days, adding a few technical skills to the training sessions, specifically for him. And fourthly, as he says later in the programme, Martin feels noticed, cared for and appreciated by the coaching staff, as he had never felt before.

If you can't discuss your performance with a superior, teacher or coach, or if you haven't got a 'superior' in the area in which you have built your Vision, you might still find it useful to discuss the results of the exercise with a friend, a relative or a colleague you trust. This way, you too might gain additional insight.

If you've followed the book's exercises so far, you will now have a Vision of your potential, you will have set specific goals, both long and short-term and, with the **skills assessment exercise**, you have taken a hard look at where you are now. There is one other step to take before composing a mental training programme to launch you on your way. As you consider where you want to be in relation to where you are now, certain obstacles to your progress will become apparent. Equally you will be able to see that you already have certain resources to call upon as you move forward. The next 4 chapters give a catalogue of possible obstacles and resources and a first introduction to the mental training exercises which can either reduce or increase their influence.

Chris Boardman – TEAM PURSUIT TEAM – July 1989

PHYSICAL SKILLS

Stamina	9	4	-5
Strength★	5	10	5
Flexibility	7	8	1
Speed★	5	10	5
Agility	9	4	-5
Balance	5	5	0
Timing	9	4	-5
Ability to relax	10	10	0
Ability to sleep	9	10	1
(Diet)			
●Food	9	10	1
●Drink	9	10	1

TECHNICAL SKILLS

Starts: in 1	8	10	2
in 2			
in 3			
in 4	9	10	1
(Changing)			
●swinging up	8	8	0
●swinging down	8	8	0
(Riding a wheel)			
●closeness	10	10	0
●ability to ride			
inside a wheel	7	4	-3
●change situation	7	7	0
●Leader Rider's			
position★	6	10	4
●Finishing	9	10	1
●Speed Control	9	10	1
●Smoothness	8	10	2
●Counting Laps	0	0	0

MENTAL SKILLS

Concentration	10	9	-1
Confidence★	6	8	2
Motivation	9	10	1
Ability to deal			
with pressure	9	10	1
(Qualities)			
●Determination	10	10	0
●Patience★	6	8	2
●Clarity	8	8	0
●Courage	10	10	0
●Ingenuity			
●Humour	9	8	-1
●Flexibility	10	9	-1
Attitudes towards:			
●Competitors	7	8	1
●Colleagues	9	9	0
●Environment	10	7	-3
●Oneself	9	10	1

Name: *CHRIS BOARDMAN*   DATE *6/7/89*

An Example of the Skills Assessment Exercise

5

Removing your inner obstacles

Having assessed your current level of skill and performance, it is time to look ahead again. Now that you know where you want to go, the hurdles you have to cross on your way will come into focus. These can be divided into two kinds – those that must be crossed within yourself, inner obstacles to your goal, and those which exist outside in the world at large.

In this chapter and the next we give a list of obstacles you may meet and the type of mental training exercised you could use to get you by each of them. Turn to a new page of your log, write 'Obstacles' at the top and note down those that you recognise in relation to your goal. After each obstacle add the names of the suggested exercises. You are still gathering information. Later, you can organise it into your own mental training programme.

Bad memories
Many different elements can trigger off bad memories – how often do you stammer and stutter in front of a particular person for what seems like no reason at all? Why do some places evoke tension and inhibit performance?

When working with sports people we frequently find that two bad performances of a particular skill are enough to cause a slump. The athlete begins to believe he can't do it right any more and as one bad memory is superimposed on another his belief is reinforced. He tells himself and then begins telling other people, 'I can't serve when it's windy' or 'I can't hole a putt from eight feet' or 'I've forgotten how to do a good boast.'

Earlier on you identified several skills – physical, technical and mental – which you feel need to be improved. What is your current dominant memory of performing each of these skills? How many of these memories are both vivid and bad?

Tottenham Hotspur Football Club failed to win a single match against Liverpool at Anfield (Liverpool's home ground) from 1912 to 1985. Although it's doubtful whether more than a few members of each year's team were seriously affected by this record, the team as a whole did tighten up whenever they were in the lead until the last twenty minutes of play. Those members of the team who had played there several years in succession without winning were affected more.

What *place* or places or type of environment give you the most problems at present? How do the bad memories of such a place block you from achieving your goal or solving your problem? Note this down.

People can also trigger off bad memories. Who bugs you most at work and how vivid is your memory of your last negative encounter with that person? How does this memory affect your current performance? Why was it that the top Swedish tennis players were for years picked off with ease by Mecir, the enigmatic Czechoslovakian player who remained many computer places lower in the world order? In a meeting do you ever get the 'Oh no, not *him* again' feeling – and know that your clarity, astuteness and power are all draining away under the table into the floor? When this happens, it is a past bad memory that has overlaid the present.

A half forgotten childhood memory of a Christmas tree suddenly covered in blazing cotton wool, set alight by tallow candles and of the burns suffered by a neighbour who hurled the whole caboodle through a smashed window and into the garden may impair the adult's judgement or at least distract their attention from a detail of importance in a future situation at work. If you are in a plane that skids off the runway and a situation which requires an emergency escape to be made, you may decide to forfeit two days holiday in order to travel to and from your next continental business appointment by train.

Bad memories of *past events* over which you had no control and even perhaps in which you had little involvement will continue to sabotage some related area of your performance until you pull them to the surface and do something with them. The first step is to unscramble the present from the past, draw out one shocking memory and dig into it to make it as clear as possible. This memory is valuable. To create change, you need to know what is holding you back.

Have a look at the list of obstacles you have noted down. Work out how it is you just 'know' in performance situations when you know things are going to go wrong?. Be as specific as you can with your answer. Is it ever a *thing* rather than a person or event? Of course it's foolish, of course it's superstitious, of course it's something you would never voice out loud but if you had to give an example, what would it be? When you've got something, focus your full attention on your answer and allow some negative memory to emerge. This pattern that your rational mind condemns as so stupid as to be worth no attention at all is blocking your progress. Examine the block with interest.

Now is the time for action. You can begin to plan a mental training programme that will diminish or transform those bad memories permanently.

Action

You should now have a complete list of bad memories that you feel have affected your performance. Now write down a full description of what happened, and what you felt. We call this 'looking at what's so' or gaining awareness and recognition. Now think of what *might* have happened, had the incident turned out as you'd have liked it to have done. Work this new version of the event into a short visualisation (**visual re-editing**) and practise it for five minutes each day for the next couple of weeks. For example, in the case of the burning Christmas tree, you might imagine the tallow candles being electric lights; or that the cotton wool was some non-inflammable material and the candles were placed correctly; or that there was water or an asbestos glove nearby and the fire was dealt with effectively without anyone being harmed.

If you then recount this visualisation out loud to a colleague or friend (**people**), being sure to say how you feel, he or she could help you to form an **affirmation**, which you could put on your bedroom wall for a couple of weeks.

Summary
Visual re-editing (p.159)
People (p.170)
Affirmation (p.142)

Negative fantasies (imagining things that aren't here)

You'll never become a world-class tennis player if you seize up every time you see a long-limbed opponent standing on the other side of the net. Let your weight go back, hit the ball tentatively and you're lost. Notice that you *imagine* this player will block out your every passing shot, you forget that in fact he or she may be slow, short-sighted, predictable or pretending not to be scared of you. All that you actually see is that he is long-limbed and is standing at the net.

When your boss strides in with a frown, holding a piece of paper and marching straight towards you, how do you react? If you hunch your shoulders and set your face, what are you imagining and how is that fantasy going to affect your interaction, perhaps even before he or she has a chance to speak? What tone are you setting for this conversation? If you were to be wrong in assuming you are going to be accused of making a mistake, what other positive interpretations might there be?

You've got your next gig coming up in a few days. That difficult, solo part still defeats you. You wait for it coming – and before you know it, your breath is short, and your fingers, normally so dexterous, feel like lumps of lead.

Inevitably, quite beyond your control, how you feel and talk an act and move depends on what you imagine not on what you see. Your reactions are usually so fast that the intermediate step goes unnoticed and unchallenged. Think of how you wish to improve your performance. What negative habitual unchallenged assumptions do you make and what is the outcome?

Action

If the long-limbed player at the tennis net causes you to seize up, begin with the **skills assessment** exercise to work out which skills you need to improve. If you find these are your forehand drive and your ability to relax, select a recent memory of a forehand drive you did well and build it into a **mental rehearsal** that you practise each day for two weeks. Then find a particular piece of **music** that makes you feel relaxed and either play it once a night for the next couple of weeks or play it through your mind as you warm-up.

If it is your interactions with the boss that are causing you trouble, compose a **mental rehearsal** of him striding towards you with a piece of paper announcing a good piece of news: the success of a project, a good deal negotiated. Rehearse your reaction at home every day for two weeks and you'll find yourself reacting positively the next time you're in a similar situation.

You've played that solo piece successfully once. Remember what it felt like – how nimbly you fingers leapt over the frets. Listen to the sound in your head. Now imagine yourself playing the same piece in the room you're going to perform in. Rehearse this regularly before the gig.

Summary
Skills assessment exercise (pp.43-54)
Mental rehearsal (p.153)
Music (p.166)

Negative self-image (thinking you are going to lose)

You may have stopped smoking for three days, three weeks or even three months but you're bound to start again sooner or later, if you think of yourself as a smoker who has given up, rather than as a non-smoker who once used to smoke. Case studies show that fat people who diet successfully usually get fat again and that the reason is that they retain an image of themselves as fat.

Before Barbara Lynch became European clay-pigeon shooting champion she told us that she could never shoot her best against world champion Canadian shooter Susan Natrass. She said that when she shot against Ms Natrass she felt smaller, less powerful and less competent. She shot accordingly.

Your self-image is a basic determinant of your performance. If your self-image is poor your performance will be poor and you'll never win through to achieving your potential. If you don't see yourself reaching your goal, you won't.

Perhaps the producer of your local dramatic society begs you to take part in his play. Terrified you reply 'I can't act. I can't possibly go on stage' even though there is a part of you that would very much like to.

In a team situation, you may restrict yourself by having a limited idea of your responsibility and therefore of your own ability. If you describe your marriage or partnership as, 'I'm the decorator, she's the cook', both members of your team are missing out individually and the team misses out as a whole. It is negative thinking, and betrays a negative self-image to say, 'I can't decorate *and* cook!'

There was a time when we were first working with Tottenham Hotspur Football Club when the strikers and midfield were at odds. The strikers claimed that the midfield didn't give them enough service, whilst the midfield claimed the strikers didn't come back sufficiently in defence. Initially, when challenged, one striker particularly held out: 'I'm a striker, not a defender!' he said: 'You can't expect me to defend *and* attack!' Of course this was the team player who was the poorest at tackling back, a skill which he subsequently improved as communication, understanding and trust improved within the team as a whole. The striker eventually gained a new self-image and became a more complete player.

Action
Many of the mental training exercises could be used to help you give up smoking. You could begin by **reading** material provided by the citizen's advice bureau. You might then have a **video** made of yourself relaxed and not smoking in a situation where you found it hard not to smoke before. You could spend time on a regular basis with a **friend** who has given up smoking and you could carry around in your purse or pocket some object that this friend gives you as a **symbol** of his/her support.

If you want to play that small part but have horrible stage fright, you could begin with two opposing exercises. First act out in front of a friend the most dreadful bout of stage fright that you can imagine, exaggerating so wildly that you both fall about laughing. Then ask the friend when it is that you **appear** most confident. Sit down, let yourself rest a moment and recapture how it feels to be you at such times.

Then get up and act the same scene as before but as if you have stepped into the scene from the confident situation without feeling any different. A further exercise would be to identify a famous actor or perhaps a politician who seems to be the epitome of confidence and find a picture of that actor to pin on your wall for a couple of days. Carry something around with you that reminds you of this person and practise acting as if you *are* that person for a few minutes, in different situations each day. Finally, you could learn the small part and **mentally rehearse** yourself performing it perfectly on stage.

Summary
Reading (p.148)
Video (p.160)
People (p.170)
Symbol (p.161)
Acting (p.168)
Picture (p.159)
Mental rehearsal (p.153)

Negative emotions

All negative emotions hinder one's ability to win, if only because they distract your attention from your objective and because they tend to expend energy that might be more usefully employed elsewhere. Emotions such as hatred, fear, scorn, greed, pride, avarice, envy and lust obstruct your ability to reach your potential.

Probably the most common hindrance is fear and anxiety, experienced at some time by all performers in every field. As a sportsperson, you may be afraid of losing, of winning, of getting injured, of losing your place in the team, even afraid of being true to yourself. If you're a team member, you may be afraid of being different in many work situations, thereby limiting and ceasing to explore your creative ability. Fear and anxiety may be a response to a real threat, an outside 'hindrance' as discussed in a moment, but just as often they are a response to what you *imagine* rather than to what is.

Of course, some emotions can both inhibit and stimulate performance. Anger, for example, can be appropriate and its expression, may, in some circumstances, be a force for the positive.

Action

Fear of flying is a response to an 'imagined' danger. To get over this, you could **read** one of the recent simple factual paperbacks on the mechanics and process of flying. You could learn some sequence of **relaxation exercises**, and develop a **quiet place** visualisation to practise eventually on take-off. You could also talk to a **friend** about a time when you were feeling completely confident and relaxed and ask him/her to help you to develop an **affirmation**, that you could repeat silently as you climb the steps into the aircraft.

Summary
Reading (p.148)
Relaxation exercises (p.167)
Quiet Place visualisation (p.156)
People (p.170)
Affirmation (p.142)

Negative patterns

It may be difficult for you to recognise which of the following patterns you possess. Some will be more apparent than others. Listen carefully to the feedback you get from others, especially things said in anger or frustration. Notice which of the patterns you find easy to recognise in other people – this can be an indication that you have a similar pattern yourself. As you identify a pattern that you need to change, note it down in your log-book – and see how often it emerges over the following few days and in what situations. How is it a pattern for you? Don't judge yourself but let it catch your interest. The more you notice, the easier it will be to build an action plan to create change. Negative patterns can be categorised in the following ways:

Sabotage thinking
Pessimism is often classified as a negative pattern or trait. If you

are a real pessimist, you'll sabotage every effort anyone makes
to help you. Asked to get a Vision, you won't have time and in
any case you add you 'are as you are' and there is no point in
believing you might change; you couldn't win anyway. Asked
to choose an ideal model, a 'hero' on which to model some
aspect of your performance for a while, you'll choose someone
worse than yourself. You'll reduce all inspirational characters to
stereotypes and you'll hide from your own inspirational quality
in the fear of being typecast yourself.

Top dog, under dog

Even if you are not a pessimist, you are sure to sabotage your
own efforts to do well, from time to time. On such occasions
there will be one part of you who says *this* is what I'm going
to do. I'll stop drinking coffee or I'll get up an hour earlier in
the morning and prepare my day properly. This part of you
will seem very definite, very strong and often very hard on
yourself. This is the part that appears to be in control. This
is the 'top dog'.

However, there is another part of yourself that says nothing
or says 'okay' when the top dog is taking decisions but, when the
time comes, proceeds to undermine all the top dog's effort. 'Oh
yes, I agree I shouldn't have coffee' and 'Yes, it's a great idea
to get up early to plan the day, but let's start the new routine
tomorrow', or 'Let's start on Monday, at the beginning of a new
week' or 'Perhaps it should be next month that I start, when I
return from holiday'. And so on.

Projection

Oscar Wilde's father, Sir William Wilde was so used to
dominating dinner party conversations that if anyone got
launched before him, he would put his head on the table and
'audibly doze'. His feeling that the speaker was long-winded
and boring was a *projection*: his own speeches were long-winded
and doubtless sometimes boring to his guests. This is another
type of negative pattern that can sabotage performance.

Everyone has a tendency to project in one circumstance or another. Projection means disowning or being blind to some part of yourself whilst being hypersensitive to that quality in others. Usually there is a 'hook' in the other person on which you hang your projection – that person does have an element of the quality you disown but usually in the other person the quality is properly integrated.

Any area of blindness to the way we operate is a hindrance to our development and our ability to win. If you want to know what quality or qualities you might have a tendency to project, think about the qualities that most upset you in other people. Listen to the way you talk about these people in this context. Do you become tense and emotional? Do you condemn in violent terms? If you hear yourself saying 'I can't *stand* people who gossip behind people's backs' or 'There you go, there you go, you're getting angry again. I'm not going to put up with it I warn you'. Listen to your tone of voice. Then step back and ask yourself, 'When did I last gossip about someone else?', or 'Is it perhaps *me* that is angry, at least as angry as he or she is?'

Introjection
When I (John Syer) first became the Scottish national volleyball coach, I made friends with the national coaches of Holland, West Germany, Italy and Czechoslovakia and spent my summer holidays at their homes, going out each day or each evening to watch them coach. In September I'd return to Scotland, get the Senior Men's team together and trot out all the drills and introduce many of the tactical systems that had so excited me abroad. I forgot that the Scottish players were nothing like the same standard. All sorts of things would go wrong. Players would make the same mistakes again and again and both they and I would get frustrated. The trouble was that I hadn't digested the new information and was trying to teach it perhaps even before I had understood all its intricacies.

This is introjection: taking in a body of information or a way of behaving without absorbing it and then bringing it out

again in undigested lumps. This behaviour can be extremely
irritating for the people you work with and create frictions
and resentments which affect your own performance. If you
are the newly-appointed departmental second-in-command in
a business organisation you can create havoc if you come out of
your boss's office on the first day and give the boss's orders as
if they were your own.

Since introjections are not part of your own instinctive self,
they tend to trap you into a set course of action, (sometimes
even into *conflicting* courses of action if you have swallowed
two conflicting concepts) and leave you fearful of and unable
to respond to changes around you. You may of course be
so unhappy in your job that you don't bother to tune in to
the structure behind the rules and regulations that govern it.
How often do we encounter someone in a large, bureaucratic
organisation who will only repeat the rules and is quite unable
to understand or is uninterested in listening to a special case?
Such a way of acting in your work cannot possibly allow you to
fully explore and express yourself. You have got yourself into
a no-win situation.

Retroflection

One of the best players in the Scottish men's volleyball
team probably never reached his potential because whenever
someone suggested some improvement to his play, his response
was to say 'Oh, I always told you I'm no good' instead of
considering, arguing and building on the idea. This was
experienced as a very subtle form of arrogance. In effect he
was not just saying 'You can't tell me anything I don't know'
but also 'I know better than you' or '*You're* no good.' If you
ever catch yourself acting in this way, you are retroflecting –
doing to yourself (in this case blaming) what you really want
to do to others. Watch out for it – it can be an easy way out.

Confluence

Confluence is not always a negative trait. When you feel

yourself fully engaged as a part of a synergistic team (a team in which the performance of the whole is greater than that capable of being produced by the sum of its parts) you can be said to feel a positive confluence with that team. So, if you are a member of a good orchestra or choir or theatre company, you will experience positive confluence as you perform.

The trait only becomes negative when you become hooked on the experience, become a 'team junkie', no longer able to discern where you end and the team begins. In team sports, the player who is in negative confluence with his team is the player who doesn't pace himself, the player who gets carried away in the first half of the match and then fades completely during the last quarter of an hour. He is also the player who never spends time on his own, who on tour has to be told to stay in his room after lunch and not even speak to his room-mate. This is the player who gets injured first because he no longer pays attention to his own needs, no longer prepares himself in the way he needs to prepare but immediately wants to warm up with others.

If you work in an office and find yourself always drawn into what other people are doing, find the open plan system enjoyable but forget what you're meant to be doing yourself, forget your own objectives within the greater whole, you are suffering from a mild state of confluence. You may overreach yourself and become ill as the pressures increase, and you certainly won't fulfil your potential or your Vision.

Neurotic competitiveness (wanting to win too badly)
Neurotic competitiveness may result from wanting to win too much. If pressures from outside or within push you to feel you have to win at all costs, you are unlikely to win in the deeper sense of fulfilling your potential and discovering what heights you may really reach in the end. As we explained in the introduction, the distinction between neurotic and creative competitiveness is that the neurotic competitor sets out to prove that he is what he feels he should be or what he feels other people

think he should be, whereas the creative competitor sets out to discover what he can do.

If you have some elements of the neurotic competitor inside you, you will discover that you limit yourself by your preconceptions and prejudgements. You can be so blinkered that you pay little attention to what happens to you and around you during competition and you often feel a wretched humiliated failure if you lose. Conversely, if you win, you probably can't help feeling that the person you have defeated is somewhat inferior to you and you may or may not like that feeling of having inflicted such a demoralisation (as you view it). At this extreme you will have become a lonely figure in chains to forces outside your control.

Goal-obsessed behaviour

The neurotic competitor usually demonstrates goal-obsessed behaviour. This you do when you forget other people and your responsibilities towards them. You forget about quality, the inner sense of rightness, harmony and order that alone ensures the perfectly created result.

You also miss unexpected opportunities and fail to notice a change of circumstances around your performance. You pay no attention to how you are doing this, sticking doggedly to methods which are no longer the most efficient. The goal-obsessed performer will never use the new computer because he or she won't take time to read the instructions.

Opposite behaviour

You may sometimes find yourself acting one way when you want to do just the opposite. You are over-assertive in a sales situation when you need to sit back and wait, or conversely, you are too uncertain when you need to drive the sale home and close. Or you are too passive during the rally and too aggressive towards the umpire when you've lost the point.

Alternatively the opposite function hasn't been developed at all. You're all skill and diplomacy, facilitating everyone

– friends, team-mates and colleagues – whereas what you really need now and then is to assert your own needs and lay claim to what is right for yourself allowing others to look after themselves. In such cases, you need to **energise the opposite**.

Most behaviour is easily categorised in polarities: active – passive, extrovert – introvert, assertive – accommodating, inclusive – exclusive, loud – soft, hard – gentle and so forth. Different situations require different qualities. It's a common misconception that you only need to be assertive, dynamic, tough and demanding to be successful. In fact, there is an equal need for consideration, skill, concern and tact. Tom Peters talks about the new style of management being 'tough and caring'.

So when everything you say or do creates a result opposite to the one you wish, bring the opposite way of expressing yourself into your performance. You may need to return to an old situation where you embodied that quality and start to build a **mental rehearsal** around that old memory. By changing the scene slowly over several sessions you can transfer the quality to your current situation and **act** it out.

Staying in the 'middle zone'

If you answer the phone and find the call is for someone else, set off to find them and then get waylaid by your manager in the corridor, you will very soon find yourself in what Gestalt calls the 'middle zone'. You don't like to interrupt but the longer your manager talks the less you can understand as you become transfixed between the need to stay where you are and the need to find the person whose phone call you've taken. You become as ineffectual as the choir member who needs to go to the lavatory but doesn't like to disturb everyone else in his or her row.

However, being in the middle zone is not just a short-or her term problem. We've worked with businessmen who want to improve their golf but find that as soon as they get on the golf course they start worrying about the work they have to do in the office. The trouble is that when they're in their office, they worry about their putting. As long as they remain in this bind, the middle zone, they do not win in either situation. It's like treading on the accelerator and the brake at the same time.

Action
A good way to begin working with negative patterns is to record their occurrence each day in your log book. Once a pattern emerges and you begin to know your top dog and under dog better or to recognise more easily the subpersonality that hovers in the middle zone, then you can do the **acting** exercise and allow the different parts of yourself to dialogue. As each side expresses its need more clearly some kind of answer or synthesis will emerge. Once again, a **friend** or colleague can provide you with feedback on your subsequent performance and you may find **pictures** to represent not just the different facets of yourself but also of the type of person you are in the process of becoming.

You may even find a **slogan** which you could put on a lapel button to express this new way of being. A good one for the top dog/under dog syndrome would be 'If all else fails, lower your standards.'

Summary
Acting (p.168)
People (p.170)
Picture (p.159)
Slogan (p.144)

Being caught in complexity

When you're under pressure or too close to a problem, it is hard to get things in perspective: you get caught up in the story or the content.

Action

At such times, just asking yourself 'what's the big picture?' is enough to step back and start examining your situation anew. We call this process 'getting the big picture'.

When we are working with clients who seem to be stuck and tying themselves in knots, we'll ask them to get up, walk over and sit in the 'observer chair' – a position from which they can 'see' themselves and the way they behave. 'All right, what do you see Joe (i.e yourself) doing that contributes to his conflict with the superintendent?', we ask . . . and often the client gets some insight that was previously missing.

Summary

Big Picture (p.136)
Empty Chair dialogue (p.169)

Distorted or Split Subpersonalities

Gurdjieff, the disconcerting Russian spiritual teacher who founded his school in Fontainebleau, Roberto Assagioli, the founder of psychosynthesis, and Carl Jung, the Swiss psychiatrist, all shared an interest in that area of human experience where psychology and spirituality overlap. All three suggested that the self you think of as 'I' has in fact many different manifestations, smaller 'I's' or, to use Roberto Assagioli's term, 'subpersonalities', each of whom has the capacity to take centre stage and act as if he or she is really you, for a certain period of time.

At work your ruler subpersonality may be dominant; in your Sunday afternoon football team it may be your joker subpersonality that emerges. The reputed hard men of English football such as Graham Roberts, Mark Dennis and Vinnie Jones may be warriors on the pitch and mystics and philosophers off it. A subpersonality is a cluster of traits – body posture, emotions, thought patterns – that crystalise around one of your potential qualities, such as power, love and judgment.

There are various ways in which a subpersonality may
be distorted. It may be involved unconsciously, expressing
hidden drives, it may have stopped growing and no longer
be appropriate for where you are now in your life; it may
work toward polarisation with other subpersonalities rather
than work in harmony as a unifying force; and it may simply
be limited and unable to express any positive quality at all.
However, at their core, there *is* a valid quality. They are trying
to meet genuine needs but, as yet, they are not doing a very good
job of it. Here are a few common distortions:

The Martyr
The Martyr is a distortion of service. It always does things for
other people but then complains that it is not appreciated.
'I work my fingers to the bone but what do *you* care', it
says.

The Critic
The Critic is a distortion of discrimination and judgement. It
is always giving negative feedback, without any appreciation
or encouragement. 'It's just not good enough', it says. Even if
someone gets a project in on time, which is just what everyone
needs and well within the budget allowed, it'll say, 'That's
fine but it's a pity you didn't include . . .', and will mention
something quite insignificant.

The Moaner
The Moaner is a distortion of the need for love. It feels the whole
world is against it and is always complaining. 'Why doesn't
anyone ever help me when I have a deadline to reach?', he
might say. Or, 'How come I'm never chosen for the first team.
The manager has got something against me, I know.'

The Controller
The Controller is a distortion of power. It has to be the boss
and it can't delegate. After telling one of its assistants to do

something, it keeps coming back to check that it's being done its way and to give fresh orders if it isn't. If it is working together with someone else on a project, it'll keep interrupting and interfering with its partner's work but won't allow his partner or anyone else to have any say in what *it's* doing.

The Mystic

The Mystic is a distortion of vision. It's an impractical dreamer who fantasises about the present and future, but never gets anything done. It's like Walter Mitty, 'All is perfect just as it is,' it might say. 'We don't really need to worry about anything. It'll work itself out . . .'

Finally, when one subpersonality works towards polarisation with another, there will be a 'subpersonality split.' Top dog versus under dog is one such split. One wanting power and the other wanting love, one wanting to achieve and the other wanting to take it easy, one wanting to be social and the other wanting to work.

As soon as one gets started, your other subpersonality feels neglected and sabotages the first one's efforts.

The result is that you go out for a meal with friends and you get miserable because another voice inside tells you you should be working. Or you go back to the office and settle down to sort out things that you've neglected for so long and you get resentful at having to be there and find you're not concentrating properly, not getting anything done. In other words, you are back in the 'middle zone'.

Action

The first exercise to turn to and follow is the **subpersonality bus** visualisation. This will allow you to identify some of your more prominent subpersonalities. Having done this you can **set goals** for the changes you wish to make. Making the inside-outside **collage** envelope and talking about this with a colleague or **friend**, will help you to sort out the distortion from the positive quality that the subpersonality represents – the martyr from the servant, the critic from the judge, the controller from the one who rules, the mystic from the visionary.

Thereafter, it would help you to find **pictures, poems** or **music** that evoked the positive quality. Put the pictures on the mantlepiece (and **dialogue** with them every so often when you are alone at home). The poetry and music, once learned, can be played through your head prior to or during important performances that you have to make.

Summary
Subpersonality Bus (p.157)
Goalsetting (p.36)
Collage (p.160)
People (p.170)
Picture (p.159)
Poetry (p.148)
Music (p.166)

Hidden quality

Sometimes a behaviour or belief hides something which you badly need. In fact, if you are dealing with a really big problem that won't go away, it may be time to review your Vision and see whether you have inadvertently built the problem in. Perhaps you are an actor who suffers from terrible first night nerves or an athlete whose nervousness makes you sick in the changing room or a concert pianist who can't sleep the night before an important concert. If so, does your Vision of a flawless performance include total calmness throughout the time before you begin? Is your reaction to try and suppress your anxiety altogether? If so, you're on the wrong track: it's nervousness and anxiety which add energy, excitement and enthusiasm to your performance.

Action
You should use this energy, instead of trying to suppress it.

Strategies for using energy are much easier than strategies for getting rid of it!

If you have a habit of losing your temper inappropriately, ask yourself, 'What is the quality behind this behaviour?' Is it aggression, assertion, a sense of rightness? Instead of suppressing the energy of your temper, discover the hidden quality and work out how to use it to enhance your performance.

Absent quality

Sometimes your progress will be blocked by having a quality or behaviour pattern in one area but not in another. You're confident at your desk but fall apart under pressure at home. You play fluent strokes from the baseline but are hopelessly tense at the net.

Action
In such cases you can learn to *transpose* the strength you have in one area to the other. **Mental imagery** will help you to work this way with such obstacles. You may have identified a lack of energy, power or discrimination as your obstacle and yet this may not always be the case. It may only occur in a certain area of your sport or in a certain area in your life. Alternatively you may recognise that you have too much of a particular quality: too much assertion, too much spontaneity. In these cases the simplest strategy is to redirect that energy to somewhere that is neglected or underdeveloped. Often you can kill two birds with one stone: relieve frustration at work by playing an aggressive game of squash. Or rechannelling some of your over hitting at the net into your service game in tennis.

Wants (chasing what you don't really need)

When you get stuck on things that you want rather than things that you really need, you have encountered another block to your ultimate success. Wants are cravings, urges and desires which are often unconscious and are not what you really need. You might want a holiday when what you need is order – going on holiday may even make things worse. You might want an affaire when what you need is a proper relationship. You might want a bar of chocolate when what you need is sympathy, love and attention.

When you chase what you want you are avoiding the real issue and can make things worse. Usually you feel some unresolved discontent which, in itself, is enough to distract you from your primary goal.

Action

Sorting out wants from needs can take time. This is the first part of the process of removing these obstacles to reaching your goal or actualising your Vision. **Goalsetting** will help you to gain a greater perspective. **Relaxation exercises** will be a step towards disidentifying from the tyranny of your wants. However, to recognise your real needs (and thereby see your wants more clearly for what they are), you might well choose to do the **Wise Old Person** visualisation.

If your need is for order rather than a holiday or sympathy rather than chocolate, you might use **music** or **poetry** to evoke the feeling or orderliness or sympathy; or you might find a model with such qualities and base an **As If visualisation** around it. In fact you may well first need to seek these qualities outside yourself and turn to **people** of your acquaintance who can meet your need and thereby release you from your want.

Summary

Goalsetting (p.36)
Relaxation exercises (p.167)
Wise Old Person visualisation (p.157)
Music (p.166)
People (p.170)
As If visualisation (p.154)

Identification with the Old (difficulty in 'letting go')

When you feel frustrated, stale or in a rut, you are probably looking at the world and behaving in a way that has become outdated. Either the world has changed around you without you paying proper attention or you have developed to a point where the old strategies don't work any more and you have to find new solutions.

Continuing with the old ways has a comforting familiarity. Change is always threatening. Yet because things are changing around you anyway, staying with the old ways of doing and looking at things becomes increasingly uncomfortable and takes you further and further off course.

Action
The obvious first steps are to discover your **Vision** and set your **goals**. From there you will probably keep a **log-book** and withdraw energy from your old patterns of behaviour by drawing **pictures** or finding pictures which represent the new. You could also use both the **Ideal model** (performance practice) and the **'As if'** visualisation, to discover the excitement and sense of accomplishment and growth that is inherent in making the change.

Dialoguing (acting) between the old and the new ways of being will also facilitate change.

Summary
Visioning (p.24)
Goalsetting (p.36)
Log-book (p.137)
Pictures (p.159)
Acting (p.168)
Ideal Model visualisation (p.153)
As If visualisation (p.154)

Being stuck in old interpretations

A hasty assumption that you understand a problem can be your first big mistake. All too often understanding means fitting your experience into the context of the past. You give meaning to your experience based upon how it compares with similar past experiences. You get information, you increase your awareness and then you immediately organise that information in terms of previous habits, previous ways of thinking, and consequently previous solutions. Once you've 'seen' the solution, you forget the problem. You become attached to the solution which takes up your entire attention.

Yet you may not have a solution to the real problem. You have a solution to the problem as you have defined it, based upon your understanding which in turn is based upon your old experience. If you always operate this way, how can you hope to recognise a new problem, never mind generate new solutions? You have formed the new in terms of the old. You have put new wine in old bottles. The result is that a new problem is disguised, a new solution is avoided and diabolically the *solution you have becomes the problem*. The solution you have reached becomes an obstacle to a solution that works.

Action
In this situation you must get rid of the solution before you can address the primary problem and generate a solution which actually creates change. In fact, you may find it useful to avoid coming to a resolution or solution at all. Keep your solution fluid by being aware of four things:

• The solution may be the problem. So challenge your solutions when you suspect they are coming from old thought patterns of the past.

• Stay in the here and now. Collect information about the past, consider how the past has helped with the present but ask questions about the here and now.

- Ask how, not why. 'Why' questions only point to what you don't know or they attempt to attribute blame without assuming responsibility. Don't ask, 'Why did you overspend your budget?' but, 'How did you overspend?' Not, 'Why did you hit it out of bounds?' but, 'How did you hit it out of bounds?'

- Avoid resolution – we don't mean don't decide or don't act. On the contrary, decisions and actions will follow the kind of understanding which isn't a knee-jerk reflex to the problem. You may need to implement containment actions: leaks in the roof need pots and pans under them *now*. An impromptu staff meeting may need some simple flipchart presentation. An unreliable fairway wood may require you to fall back on your irons. However, when the emergency is over, you must look for solutions that address the root cause and introduce change in the system.

Previous solutions

Identification with the old usually includes attempting to solve problems in a way that is no longer working. In fact it can even be that it is your solution which itself is the block to progress. If your objective for instance is to fall asleep as soon as you go to bed at night, your efforts to fall asleep – whether counting sheep or drinking herb tea with the intention of falling asleep early – are in fact keeping you awake.

Another example of the solution being the problem, given in Paul Watzlawick's book *The Language of Change* is of the mother who tries to get her son to stop sucking his thumb, first by threatening, then by punishing and even by shaming him but to no avail: the child was receiving the attention he needed, even though the attention was expressed negatively.

The more his mother threatened, the more the child felt her attention to be hooked on him.

Action
The action to remove this obstacle differs from others. Although you might be taking quite logical steps in trying to solve it, you are actually focusing on the wrong thing. The way to remove this obstacle is primarily to stop trying to remove it: it is the way in which you are trying to remove it that ensures it stays in place.

As soon as you try to stay *awake*, instead of trying to go to sleep, you feel the first signs of tiredness. The mother who was inadvertently satisfying her son's need for attention by threatening him with punishment for sucking his thumb, discovered that she reached her objective by telling her son to suck not just his thumb but each of his fingers as well, for an equal amount of time, and to report to her each day as he did it.

It may not be easy to let go of old solutions but, beginning with a **relaxation** and perhaps continuing by asking your **Wise Old Person** how your solution might be the problem and what the opposite approach might be, would help. You might also brainstorm on alternative or indeed opposite solutions, ways of restating the obstacle, with two or three colleagues or **friends**.

Summary
Goalsetting (p.36)
Relaxation exercises (p.167)
Wise Old Person visualisation (p.157)
People (p.170)

Insufficiently developed skills

The **skills assessment** exercise described earlier, will have helped you to identify those physical, technical and mental performance skills which you need to improve. The insufficient level of skill in certain aspects of your performance is bound to hinder your ability to win. If the exercise has shown that you believe your diet is poor then it is your diet that needs to be improved. If you realised that you are unable to relax but that it is important to relax if you are to perform well, then your tension will be blocking your progress.

Look too at the mental skills column. Which of the listed qualities score high? Do your scores suggest that you get too aggressive, that you are too impatient or too rigid in your outlook, that you lack a sense of lightness and humour? If so, you will need to work with these qualities as well.

Action
Start with your **Vision** and **goalsetting** to get clear which skills are most required, then do the **skills assessment** exercise to see which of the required skills you consider to be least developed. Thereafter your mental training programme may include almost any of the mental training exercises, although a **mental rehearsal** of a good past performance, and an **affirmation**, developed from that rehearsal, should probably be part of it.

Summary
Goalsetting (p.36)
Skills assessment exercise (p.43-54)
Mental rehearsal (p.153)
Affirmation (p.142)

6

Removing
outside obstacles

It is interesting to note that this chapter is much shorter than the last one. It seems that the obstacles within confuse our Vision and interrupt our progress more than any outside factors. That said, you are unlikely to realise your Vision without encountering challenges from the world around you.

Do as before: read through the chapter, noting down those hurdles or obstacles that you recognise as being in your path right now. Add the names of the suggested mental training exercises after each of these obstacles, so that you may construct your own training programme later on.

Stressors

Stressors are an outside disturbance or threat to your performance. Stress itself is your reaction to being disturbed, which may be either positive or negative. Stressors are therefore *potential* obstacles.

John Adams, in an early article on stress management*, distinguished between stressors in the form of *recent* events and *on-going* events; and between events *at* work and events *away from* work – work being the place of performance.

*'Improving Stress Management: An Action-Research based on Intervention', W W Burke (ed.), *The Cutting Edge* University Associates, 1978

Stressors you may encounter as recent events at work (designated Type 1 by John Adams) are a major change of instructions, policies or procedures, the need to stay late to get your work completed, an increase in the volume of your work, a new superviser, co-worker or subordinate, or a complete change of job.

Stressors you may encounter as recent events away from work (Type 2) are marriage, moving house, birth of child, death of a relative or friend and illness.

Stressors you may encounter as on-going events at work (Type 3) are too much work and too little time in which to do it, feedback only when you are wrong, conflict between sections, unclear standards and responsibilities, role ambiguity, lack of participation, interpersonal conflict, territoriality, too many deadlines, a lack of social support, a lack of confidence in your manager, always fire-fighting instead of working to a plan, having to go to unnecessary meetings, being interrupted all the time, ambiguities, poor delegation and poor communications.

Finally, stressors that you may encounter as on-going events away from work (Type 4) are pollution, noise, financial worries, family problems and being unable to fit in with your social milieu.

Action

Free writing – ten minutes of uncorrected, uncensored scribble – is an exercise that can both help you to identify the source and effect of the stressors which are inhibiting your performance and suggest how you may recreate the experience into productivity.

Thereafter you might build some programme of **relaxation** and breathing exercises, decide to put the stresssors temporarily into the visualised **Black Box**, develop a **Quiet Place** visualisation and employ a number of methods such as **trigger books**, **music**, **pictures** and **poetry** to pull you back on to course when your old reactions threaten to return.

Summary
Free writing (p.147)
Relaxation exercises (p.167)
Black Box visualisation (p.155)
Quiet Place visualisation (p.156)
Trigger book (p.149)
Music (p.166)
Picture (p.159)
Poetry (p.148)

Other people

A manager you don't trust, co-workers with whom there is friction, and subordinates who are new to their job are all potential hindrances to you achieving your potential or your goal. How far or how long other people are really able to block you is debatable but what we imagine can be as powerful as what is.

Action
You may experience someone or some other people as being distractions and obstacles to actualising your Vision or realising your goal. If so, it is as well to begin by stepping back and re-assessing your goal, looking particularly at your chosen action steps. You may find alternative action steps fit better into your current situation or you may just find it helps you to get back on course. It is a good exercise to make a list of all the people who you feel are obstacles and detail how you see each one hindering you.

Thereafter, you have a choice of exercises that can help you to establish the needs of both yourself and the person or people concerned and to distinguish these needs from co-existing wants. You could begin by looking at your own wants and needs, doing the **Subpersonality Bus** visualisation and seeing which subpersonalities appear and what they have to say. You might then turn your attention to your mode of interaction

with the person or people whom you perceive to be obstacles
and **dialogue** with them, imagining them on the empty chair
opposite you and **acting** out an exchange as you move back and
forth between the two chairs.

Alternatively, you might do the **Quiet Place visualisation**
and then mentally invite the person to visit your quiet place
and 'dialogue' with you there, telling you his real needs and
helping you to find a way to accommodate them. Write down
your memory of this discussion in your log book or describe it
to a **friend** or colleague, so that you can develop an **affirmation**
that will help you to stay on your new course.

Summary
Goalsetting (p.36)
Subpersonality Bus visualisation (p.157)
Acting (p.168)
Quiet Place visualisation (p.156)
Log-book (p.147)
People (p.170)
Affirmation (p.142)

Isolation

Living and or working alone may be an obstacle to your
development. Despite the time and energy that may appear
to be lost in conflict and the accommodation of the needs of
others, other people are an invaluable resource. Above all,
isolation denies you feedback and a source of creative conflict
or competition.

Action
You might begin reducing this obstacle by using your **journal**
to explore your feelings. List the advantages and disadvantages
of your isolation in your log-book, including in the disadvantages
of lack of feedback and lack of creative conflict. Reflect on
ways in which you might meet your needs differently and

then review the whole process by reevoking your **Vision** and revising your goals and action steps in a new **goalsetting** exercise.

Having done all this and found that a certain measure of isolation (over and above its positive contribution towards your success) is inevitable, look at ways in which you can compensate. You can get information and new ideas by **reading** material written by others or watching technical **videos**. Or you can consult your own intuition through the **Wise Old Person** visualisation or through **drawing**.

You can get feedback through writing down your ideas and sending them to **people** who are willing to help. You might find encouragement and inspiration in **music**, **autobiographies**, **poetry** or a **picture**.

Summary
Journal (p.147)
Visioning (p.24)
Goalsetting (p.36)
Reading (p.148)
Videos (p.160)
Wise Old Person visualisation (p.157)
Drawing (p.159)
People (p.170)
Music (p.166)
Poetry (p.148)
Picture (p.159)

Environment

Is there anything about your environment at 'work' or at home, not mentioned under 'Stressors' which you experience as a hindrance or obstacle to your progress? Do you have sufficient space, silence, light, warmth and protection from the elements? (Do you have too much?)

Action

Again, where you perceive the environment as being an obstacle, begin by writing – in a personal **journal** first, if it is an emotional issue, or straight into your log book – establishing which elements in the environment hinder you and which in fact might help. With all outside obstacles you should first see what is in your power to change and then, with those things you cannot or choose not to change, you find a way to alter your attitude towards them.

If we run a mental training workshop for coaches and athletes and find that the room is in a noisy sports complex, we first ask the group to recognise that everyone in the building is either practising, performing or administering sport and that we are all part of this sports 'family'. We might then run an exercise on improving concentration and welcome the noise as a means of practising.

Many of the same mental training exercises used to reduce other outside obstacles can help reduce the apparently negative effects of your environment. **Relaxation exercises** followed by a **Quiet Place visualisation** will help you to withdraw from the situation periodically and regain composure or recharge your energy supply. **Mental rehearsal** of a new response to the environment, backed up by an **affirmation** will also help. You can then chose **pictures** and **music** to reinforce this response.

Summary
Journal (p.147)
Relaxation exercises (p.167)
Quiet Place visualisation (p.156)
Mental rehearsal (p.153)
Affirmation (p.142)
Picture (p.159)
Music (p.166)

Objects

Actual as well as remembered objects may obstruct your progress. Perhaps some tool of your trade is outdated, inappropriate or even dangerous to use. A boy may get hooked on the game of tennis whilst teaching himself with an old slackly strung wooden frame racket but for him to progress further and reach his potential he will need one that is the correct weight and balance.

Or you might be trying to play Debussy's *Syrinxe* on a flute on which even 'Three Blind Mice' would be difficult. Nor is writing the greatest 20th-century novel on granny's old typewriter with its sticky keys particularly easy!

Action
Again, you might start by writing a list in your **log-book** not just of the disadvantages of the object that is inhibiting your performance but also its advantages. If this is difficult, search your memory for someone who would respond positively to the situation and model your own response and behaviour on his or hers, during five minute periods of **As If visualisation**.

If you still feel blocked **read** all you can about this object, discover where it comes from, how it works, what its nature is: 'make friends with it' if you like. John Betjeman, the English poet laureat, realising how drained he was by his hatred of traffic noise and fumes – that his hatred caused him more damage than the noise and the fumes combined – spent part of each day for several weeks, learning all he could about cars.

You could also explore what the offending object symbolises for you by 'inviting' it to your **Quiet Place** and dialoguing with it there or 'putting' it on the empty chair and **acting** out a dialogue between yourself and the object. Having discovered the part that the object touches in you, you can use **mental rehearsal** and any of the evocative exercises – **mascots, rituals, collages, pictures, affirmations** – to effect a healing and reconciliation. If, perhaps to your surprise, you discover that the object being broken distresses you more than it does other people, you might move on to the memory of some particularly traumatic moment in the past when something broke. In this case, you could begin to heal the memory and move back to an easier acceptance of the present through constructing and practicing a **Visual re-editing** visualisation.

Summary
As If visualisation (p.154)
Reading (p.148)
Quiet Place visualisation (p.156)
Acting (p.168)
Mental rehearsal (p.153)
Mascot (p.164)
Ritual (p.165)
Collage (p.160)
Picture (p.159)
Affirmation (p.142)
Visual re-editing (p.159)

7

Maximising
your strengths

Now you have a clear picture of the obstacles to realising your Vision or achieving your goal, turn your attention to your resources. Where can you go for help? What positive forces are there at hand that could support you in your efforts?

You should start by identifying your inner strengths. Consider each in turn and write them down in your log book. After each strength that you recognise, list the mental training exercises that may be used as reinforcement.

Your Vision

Your Vision has the power to summon your strengths and galvanise you into action. The clearer and better the Vision, the greater the course of energy.

Once you have outlined your Vision, it is a potential source of inspiration at times when you feel trapped, in a rut or overwhelmed by the demands of your daily routine. Your Vision should be referred to regularly, explored and expanded. It should also be tied down.

Action
The first task is to set **goals**, with your Vision firmly in your sights and then to establish an action plan. What step can you take towards your goals, in line with your Vision, this

week? Once out of your rut and into the new groove, build the ramparts to ensure you stay pointed in the right direction. Keep a record of your performance in your log book, as you work towards achieving your one-month goals. Develop a **ritual** attuned to your new intentions. This ritual may include a daily **relaxation** session followed by a **mental rehearsal** of actualising your Vision and of actions you will take on the way.

What will be the quality of your behaviour as you reach your objective? If you find an image that represents that quality, you can develop an **As If visualisation** and act that way for a short time each day.

Contemplating your Vision and describing it to a **friend** or colleague, you can develop an **affirmation** that will guide you through times of challenge and confusion. At the same time you might find a **mascot**, some object that evokes your intention. This should be an object you can touch, hold or even secretly talk to (as Greg Lougarnis the World and Olympic Champion diver talked to his teddy bear). It's 'stupid' of course, but effective nonetheless.

Summary
Goalsetting (p.36)
Log-book (p.147)
Ritual (p.165)
Relaxation exercises (p.167)
Mental rehearsal (p.153)
As If visualisation (p.154)
People (p.170)
Affirmation (p.142)
Mascot (p.164)

Your memory and imagination

If memories of past failure are potential hindrances to your progress, memories of *past successes* can help. The more vivid the memory the better – and vivid means remembering not just what you could see but what you could hear, what you were touching, what you could smell and sometimes even what you could taste. Usually the most important sense however is how it *felt* to perform that way, memory of your posture or of the way that you moved. When you evoke such a memory you are consulting your kinaesthetic sense. A detailed memory of the environment in which you performed, of the atmosphere, of other people present is also valuable.

If you have no memory at all of performing successfully the skill that you now wish to improve, you will have other memories of success either of the same skill in a different situation or of a different skill in the same situation. These memories are also valuable, as are memories of having seen *someone else* perform the skill successfully.

Places can also evoke strong memories. Your mind is a library with innumerable shelves from which you can pull down memories appropriate to any present performance need. You will have memories of quiet places, memories of safe places, memories of exotic places, memories of places that are neat and orderly. You will have memories of places that are warm, of places that are cool, of places in the spring, summer, autumn and winter – all of which give you a positive feeling of one sort or another.

Other people, too, can be a source of inspiration. A moment's reflection will allow you to recall people displaying a whole range of positive qualities, each of which will be helpful to you in developing specific aspects of your performance. You'll have memories of purity, clarity, honesty, goodness, humour, wisdom, generosity, patience, straightforwardness, courage, flexibility, honour and of all the other qualities you consider important in achieving your aim. Select the memory or memories which make a direct connection with your current objective.

You will also have memories of other people performing technical and physical skills which you may not have perfected yet yourself. These too are valuable resources.

Positive memories of *past events* are equally valuable. They allow you to access a particular feeling – emotional or kinaesthetic – which is tied to the past occasion. Evoking such memories can be the easiest way to access such feelings. So turn to a different shelf of your library and cast your eye along the historical sequence of events you have witnessed or experienced, which aroused some strong positive feeling in you. Run through memories – perhaps of your mother combing your hair, of a Christmas morning, of being helped to build a boat by your father, of a great procession, of playing truant with a close friend, of an early love affair, of your team's triumph. Somewhere amongst your vast collection will be a memory to help you now.

You'll have intense and positive memories too of loved animals, of cherished trophies, of comfortable old clothes. You'll have memories of films and books, of toys and ornaments, of an old typewriter or a cracked mug – in the words of the Frank Sinatra song 'these foolish things.' Review them not for a sense of nostalgia but to discover a resource that can convey the sense that you are able to move forward and achieve what you want to achieve now.

It makes no difference whether the safe place, strong person or inspiring event that you use to help you is real, remembered or imagined: imaginary examples will work just as well. If someone told you as a child, in a voice that implied you were a liar, that you had a 'vivid imagination', throw that particular memory in the waste basket: your imagination is an invaluable resource and should be cultivated.

Note down now in your log-book, places, events, people or pictures that might help you. These can all be built in to your mental training programme.

Action
Your memory and your imagination are the source of constructed visualisation by which you may improve your performance and achieve your goal. Memories and fantasies are

unstructured and either arise randomly or are triggered by some present factor or occurence. Visualisation is a method of deliberately constructing and practising in the positive aspects of your memories and imagination, to practise and determine your response to the future.

Select clips of certain appropriate positive memories of past action and practise these **mental rehearsals** regularly for five minutes a day for a couple of weeks. Half-remembered memories of high or peaceful places may be etched out with piercing clarity by your imagination and become well-rehearsed, instantly available and intensely personal versions of the **Wise Old Person** or **Quiet Place** visualisations.

The mental rehearsals can be further secured by **affirmations** that arise from their description, the positive expression of emotional and kinaesthetic feeling that is constructed into a sentence that begins with the pronoun 'I' and is in the present tense. Your **Quiet Place** or the experience of meeting the **Wise Old Person** may be made more instantly available through **drawing** or composing **poetry** or finding an object (a **symbol**) which evokes the experience.

Summary
Mental rehearsal (p.153)
Wise Old Person visualisation (p.157)
Quiet Place visualisation (p.156)
Affirmation (p.142)
Drawing (p.159)
Poetry (p.148)
Symbol (p.161)

Your dreams

Your waking dreams will have a close and enlightening connection with your Vision. Summon them, express them in prose, poetry or pictorial form and use them as powerful tools for achieving your Vision. Your sleeping dreams are elusive, illogical, frustrating, scary, hilarious or strange. They are also a gift.

Allow yourself to capture your dreams in the belief that they express the answer you seek. Nobody can tell you what your dreams mean – indeed, your dreams don't mean anything – but if you ascribe meanings to your dreams, they may provide you with inspiration and the answer you seek.

For most people dreams are an untapped resource. We turn away from them in haste to the comfortable familiarity and incessant demands of our daily routine. 'What use is such nonsense?' we might ask. They *are* disturbing. As we write this, the train we are travelling on stops at a Swiss mountain village. On the platform, beneath a low slanted roof stands a bespectacled official. His peaked cap slants parallel to the roof and behind him is a sign that says 'ZUOZ'. This is the stuff of dreams, the start of a novel or film that could go anywhere.

Your Vision, the Vision you've constructed from your waking dreams, should never be allowed to restrict you. Your Vision is a source of inspiration, able to lift you from the predictable safe routine of the present towards a new reality. The path should be one of discovery. Perhaps at a different level, at a point further along the path, what seems chaotic now will be seen to have order (and a *new* level of chaos will be there for you to experience.) The often unpalatable but challenging truth is that life is not meant to be comfortable. It's meant to be exciting. We are here to move into the unknown and struggle towards our potential. Paradox, riddles and dreams all offer an escape route from the false 'Vision prison'.

Action

Keep your journal beside your bed for a week or two. Write down the dreams you remember as you wake. Capturing them may seem difficult at first. If so, stop saying, 'I can't remember my dreams' or 'I *never* dream.' Begin saying, 'I can't quite remember what I dreamed last night' and scraps of dreams will stay with you long enough to write them down. As the week goes by, if you continue to make the effort, the scraps will become longer and more complete.

You might also spend a week or two noting down the thoughts that come into your mind as you drift towards sleep – though this requires more dedication. These images and sentences are called 'hypnogogic experiences'. If you have an office of your own or a private place at work, and can take a very brief catnap in the middle of the day, allow yourself to rest and contact this expression of your mind, especially on days filled with pressure and unresolved problems.

You could join a Gestalt group or a Jungian dream group to gain extra impetus to remember. Such a group will also allow you to gain new insight into your current performance and your path towards your Vision, by giving you the opportunity to **act** out parts of a dream. Perhaps you dream that you climb up some stairs you've never noticed before, into an attic with cobwebs, shining green apples, old trunks and something strange wrapped up in faded cloth, pushed into one corner. A door opens and in comes the station master. 'This is FTAN' he says and the atmosphere of the room behind him makes your skin prickle. So *be* the station master, *be* the apples, *be* the room behind the station master and talk to the attic. *Be* the thing in the corner of the room and talk to the cobwebs. Each part of the dream expresses a part of yourself and by acting out such dialogues you discover new dimensions and resources of your being.

If you are alone, you might do a **relaxation exercise**, reflect on a particularly striking dream or fragment of a dream, and then do the **Wise Old Person** visualisation. When you meet your Wise Old Person, ask what quality this dream represents and how you might best use this quality to further your cause.

You may also **draw** what seems to be an important recurring dream and describe your drawing to others; or you may, as Coleridge did in *The Ancient Mariner*, express it in a **poem**. In doing this you will discover some new quality that you can use to help you reach your objective. For instance, acting out parts of your dreams may well help you to get in touch with your creativity and power. Such an experience may then often be captured and reevoked by formulating an **affirmation**.

Summary
Journal (p.147)
People (p.170)
Acting (p.168)
Relaxation exercises (p.167)
Wise Old Person visualisation (p.157)
Drawing (p.159)
Poetry (p.148)
Affirmation (p.142)

Your intuition

As you grow to appreciate your unique character and experience you develop a trust in your own sensitivity, to the voice within or your 'Higher Self'. It might help initially to think of the you who appreciates the chance to withdraw and reflect as a *part* of yourself, a subpersonality if you like, who is often in conflict with the part of you who expresses a compulsive need to act and interact with others.

Action
Make a deal with the compulsive 'you' and take five minutes a day to be alone and reflect, to be still, to meditate and to hear the voice of your intuition. Programming a time of silence will strengthen your ability to trust your intuition in times of crisis.

The more established this practice becomes, the greater the depth of your understanding and the calmer and more confident you will be. You learn to pace yourself. Instinctively you withdraw, when to stay with the crowd is to become an aimless passenger. You return restored and able to contribute fully.

Making clear to yourself your own needs is a basic function of your intuition, analogous to checking the petrol gauge, the oil level, tyre pressure and water tank of your car to ensure it continues to get you safely to your destination. However, your intuition is also capable of informing you what you should do and where you should be at any moment. One of the most astonishing people either of us have ever met is Peter Caddy, an ex-army officer and co-founder of the Findhorn Foundation. When we knew him, Peter would often detach himself abruptly from a deep conversation in which he was fully involved, saying 'I have to go now. I need to be at . . . [such and such a place].' The place might have been a hundred yards or a hundred miles away but he was almost always right: he *did* need to be there. Peter has an ability similar to that required of all great athletes, the ability to switch his full attention from outside to inside himself and back at a moment's notice.

Your intuition then, is capable of telling you things you don't realise you need to know. It also has the ability to give solutions to problems which have long been a pain. For this too you need first to **relax** and to allow your mind to rest (which is difficult) and become conscious of the way it chatters on.

One good way to do this is **free writing**, an exercise designed to move a 'writers block' but equally proficient at suggesting escape routes from circular problems. It achieves this precisely by allowing you to watch how your mind works. You get two or three sheets of paper, an egg-timer and a pen. Having relaxed and reviewed your problem, you turn the egg-timer over and begin tc write fast, simply watching what appears on the page without judgement, without any alteration whatsoever, without even going back to check punctuation. As the last grain of sand falls from the top of the egg-timer to the bottom, you stop, put down your pen and read over what you have written. And somewhere amongst all the nonsense will be the germ of an idea.

Other ways to touch into your intuition are to go to your **'Quiet Place'**, get an image for your problem and invite your problem in this guise to visit you. Once it is there, in your Quiet Place, you dialogue with it, enquiring what it is that it needs. Alternatively you can walk up your mountain and put the problem to your **Wise Old Person**, who – as you'll discover after practising the exercise for a while – actually *is* your intuition.

Certainly your intuition is a right-brain faculty, which involves 'thinking of' your problem rather than 'thinking about' it. It's fairly obvious then that **drawing** your problem and looking at it anew from this different perspective can also work.

Summary
Relaxation exercises (p.167)
Free writing (p.147)
Quiet Place visualisation (p.156)
Wise Old Person visualisation (p.157)
Drawing (p.159)

Your rational intelligence

Although it may often restrict you or, if based on false premises, may lead you astray, your rational intelligence can be an immense resource when attempting to overcome doubts and fears or other irrational emotions. Your ability to think *about* something may have been developed only at the expense of your ability to think *of* it but don't right the balance by discarding your ability to think straight. Perfect your ability to 'think of' whilst retaining your ability to 'think about'. Then, in addressing the challenge of meeting your goal, shuttle from one to the other.

Action
To reinforce your rational intelligence you need clarity and order, space and time. For some people this may mean tidying their desk, spring-cleaning the house, or putting old socks in the clothes basket. For others it may mean leaving the house altogether and going for a long walk; for others again it may

mean seeking out a **person** they respect, making a pot of tea and settling back in an armchair to talk.

Goalsetting and assessing your current level of skill, serve to clear the decks mentally and make a new start. Going to the reference library or **reading** through old files may provide the background information you need, as may questioning your boss, your coach or a knowledgeable peer. Planning a tactical approach and **writing** your plan down or telling a close friend of your intentions will reinforce your ability to hold to a rational line. **Reviewing** your performance at each stage, by searching out and recording some small success – even when you feel ashamed of what seems a total failure – will give you a sense of progress. It will reinforce your ability to stand back and use your basic intelligence as you make renewed efforts.

In fact your rational intelligence is a major arm in your artillery when dealing with debilitating emotion. You best reinforce your intelligence by establishing a routine that includes time put aside for its use. Notice what time of day you analyse best – before anyone else gets up, before anyone else gets to the office, after everyone else has left – and make sure that you are free and relatively refreshed at that time. Discover where you think logically best and who with. It may be a seat in your garden, the middle table of a local reference library, your desk at home or at work or your car on the motorway with a Brandenburg Concerto playing in the background.

If you are going through a phase when you're liable to say, 'I never get time to think!', you could reinforce your rational ability by doing a **mental rehearsal**. Think back to a time when you *were* unhurried and astute in your assessment of situations. Think of a particular moment, rehearse where you were, what you were doing and how you felt both physically and emotionally. Then practise that rehearsal once a day for a couple of weeks and formulate an **affirmation** or identify a piece of **music** which will evoke this feeling over the same period of time. In this way you are constructing a mental training programme to reinforce your rational intelligence.

Summary
People (p.170)
Goalsetting (p.36)
Skills assessment exercise (pp.43-54)
Reading (p.148)
Preparation and review (p.141)
Writing (p.147)
Mental rehearsal (p.153)
Affirmation (p.141)
Music (p.166)

Your will

As a further inner resource you have willpower to back your use of rational intelligence. There are three types of will: strong will, skillful will and goodwill. Strong will is expressed by putting your head down, pushing through obstacles and staying up half the night to meet a deadline. Skillful will is expressed by organising your resources ahead of time, using just the right amount of energy to ensure things get done, sitting in a comfortable chair to make a few phone calls instead of rushing out to do things.

Finally goodwill is expressed by making things work for other people, being of service, helping others. If you sent money to Russia to help the Armenian earthquake survivors you were expressing goodwill. When we turned round at the end of a course we had run for Manufacturing Education and Training at Ford Motor Company (Europe), to our surprise we found three members of the Department had come to help us pack up. These three were expressing their goodwill.

Action
Strong will can be reinforced by **goalsetting** and **preparation and review**. It can be further reinforced by telling colleagues or team mates of your goals and tactics and by relating your

Vision to **friends**. Whilst a football team may have a trophy on the dressing-room table to stoke their determination, your **symbol** might be something as old fashioned and simple as a knot in the corner of your hankerchief. (If you use tissues, tie a double knot in one shoe lace. If you wear loafers, put your watch in your pocket or wear it on the wrong wrist!)

Skilful will may also be reinforced by **preparation and review** but if you have a tendency to charge at your objective like a bull at a red rag, find an **image** for skilfulness. Who for you is a skilful **person**, who gets things done with a minimum of fuss? Go and spend time with that person, act 'as if' you are that person for five minutes each day, do a **mental rehearsal** of a time when you saw them act that way (change that rehearsal into one in which you become that person – an **ideal model visualisation**) and find a **picture** of them to stick on your bedroom wall for the two weeks or so that you work to reinforce this particular quality.

Goodwill expresses love or caring, an optimal quality of any coach or team leader but also a quality possessed by the self-motivated athlete, the athlete secure enough in himself to give rather than take and who is always concerned to demonstrate and pass on personal experience to younger members of the team. In the best teams members learn to express goodwill early. All members learn from the examples set by the team leader and by senior members, so that the expression of goodwill becomes a norm. Indeed, seeking the company of other **people** within a team is one way to discover and reinforce the goodwill you already have.

If you do the **Subpersonality Bus** exercise or you dialogue with aspects of a recurrent dream and discover that you readily identify with a grasping possessive part of yourself, attempt to discover the needs of this subpersonality that exist behind its wants. In all probability you'll discover a need for security and confidence. If so, invite the subpersonality to your **Quiet Place** and ask what would help it to feel more secure. (In doing this you may realise that you the observer, you who can rest and enjoy your Quiet Place *is* confident and secure and is able to express goodwill towards others). When you have an answer you may make a contract with the possessive subpersonality whereby you will take steps to secure for it its real need.

If you prefer a 'thinking about' analytical left-brain approach, do a **skills assessment** exercise to determine in which aspects of your performance you are in fact confident and which aspects are least developed and therefore most responsible for your insecurity. You then devise a programme of technical and mental training exercises – perhaps physical ones too – which will develop those weaker skills. The mental training exercises will include remembering a past good performance of that particular skill and building the memory into a **mental rehearsal**, getting an **affirmation** from a verbal description of that performance, finding an object or **symbol** of that performance and even a **picture** or piece of **music** that evokes that performance. An affirmation, symbol, picture and a piece of music might also be used directly to evoke the experience of your own goodwill.

Summary
Goalsetting (p.36)
Preparation and review (p.141)
People (p.170)
Symbol (p.161)
Image (p.161)
As If visualisation (p.154)
Mental rehearsal (p.153)
Subpersonality Bus (p.157)
Quiet Place visualisation (p.156)
Skills assessment exercise (pp.43-54)
Affirmation (p.141)
Music (p.166)
Picture (p.159)

Your appreciation

A sports person has a coach, a student has a teacher, anyone moving into a new job has someone to show them the ropes. Those that learn fastest are those who are given appreciation and an indication that the instructor has their best interests at heart. In psychosynthesis terms, the good instructor shows both will and love. As Gabriella Sabatini's coach, Patricio Apey once said, 'There has to be a lot of love for a young player to develop.'

Using this book as a guide to improving your performance, you are on your own. That's fine but don't be shy of appreciating the effort you are making, of celebrating each success. When the time is right, give yourself a break, a rest, a snooze, a holiday. If you listen to yourself, learn and respect your personal rhythms, you'll know that you deserve it.

Your love and appreciation, your ability to recognise strength of intention and each small success of others as well as of yourself is a powerful inner resource.

Action
Goodwill that you demonstrate towards others is reflected back to you and ultimately enhances your own performance. The same is true of appreciation. Failure to appreciate yourself can affect not just your own performance but also the performance of others, as you lapse into retroflection or insecurity and even possessiveness.

To reinforce your ability to appreciate yourself, begin again with the **skills assessment** exercise, which will remind you which skills you are well pleased with, skills in fact that you may perform better than many colleagues or opponents. Then do a daily **review** of your performance, in the light of the objectives and tactics you decided upon during your **preparation**. As you appreciate yourself more objectively and without false modesty, your preparation will become more appropriate as you relate your plan or tactics to your current strengths.

Review your best performances visually as well as verbally, selecting key moments for future **mental rehearsal** exercises. Listen to your family, **friends** and team mates, if you are part of a team. They may be able to teach you to see yourself more objectively and may reflect or spark off in you a thought that can become an **affirmation**.

Finally try being kind to your body and see how soon this practice affects your performance for the better. Give yourself time each day to do a five-minute **relaxation** and note down its effect and the thoughts and feelings it arouses, in your log-book.

Summary
Skills assessment exercise (pp.43-45)
Preparation and review (p.141)
Mental rehearsal (p.153)
People (p.170)
Affirmation (p.142)
Relaxation exercises (p.167)
Writing (p.147)

Your well-developed performance skills

Between performances – between a weekly meeting with your boss and the next or between one important sales attempt and another – like the footballer, you might withdraw, get a perspective on your current level of ability and work (as the footballer trains) to improve your weaker skills. Come the moment of your next performance, your objective changes from specific improvement to being as successful as you can. In other words, there are times when you play to your strengths. If you have a flamboyant manner that works for you at least 80% of the time and a quiet and patient act that has never worked yet, you may follow a mental training programme to improve your patient act between sales but, for the time being, at least you continue to rely on your flamboyance when your immediate goal shifts to making a successful sale today.

If your attitude towards your opponents is suspect, if you easily allow yourself to be riled by humorous jibes, but you always make the best of your environment, then switch your attention to all there is in the environment that supports you, whenever you feel yourself rising to the bait. After the deal is completed and you can withdraw again, switch your objective back to improving your attitude towards your 'opponents' and work at your mental training programme again. Next week you may have strengthened this skill enough to allow you to use it a little on the day.

Action

You make the most of these resources by establishing which of your performance skills are the most effective, by doing the **skills assessment** exercise. Then you can build use of the skills you have identified into the action step programme of a renewed one-month **goalsetting** exercise. Finally, having set your goals and worked out your tactics, you can **plan** for each day's programme, going through the physical, emotional and mental routine that works best for you.

If the **skills assessment** exercise gives you any surprises, remind yourself of the improvements that you have made recently by formulating an **affirmation** or finding an appropriate **photograph** of yourself and sticking it up on the wall for a couple of weeks. Make sure you use your performance skills effectively by reading chapter nine on preparation.

Summary
Skills assessment exercise (pp.43-54)
Goalsetting (p.36)
Preparation (p.141)
Affirmation (p.142)
Picture (p.159)

8

Maximising outside support

Having identified your inner strengths and included reinforcement exercises into your mental training programme, take a look at the resources you have available around you. What or who is there to help you further towards your objective?

Read through the following suggestions. Note down in your log book those that strike a chord and after each, list the exercises that can reinforce this support.

Other individuals

Consider your goal in relation to the range of your friends, family, colleagues, aquaintances and people of whom you've heard but never met. Other individuals can be a source of information, ideas, feedback, practical help, provocation, inspiration and comfort. In their presence you will often be able to step back from your performance and gain a clearer perspective.

Other people can be useful models. Who is good at the aspect of your performance that you want to improve? Spend time with them, watch and listen. If you want to improve your ability to relax or to visualise or to tune in more clearly to your intuition and inner wisdom, what discipline would help – yoga? painting? music? – and who would be the best teacher or specialist for you, from whom you could learn?

Other people are there to be approached. A coach in charge of many athletes may not always tune in as well as he or she should to the needs of each one. Sometimes the athlete must knock on the coach's door to get personal information and guidance. Consult your needs, look around you and do the same.

Action

How can you make full use of people as a resource? First you must be clear about what precisely you need. The basic **goal setting** exercise will help you, provided you move on from goals to action steps: it is the second part of the exercise which ties down *how* you are going to achieve your goal and in this case that means – when will you pick up the telephone to arrange a meeting?

Having made an appointment to meet this person, sit down and do your mental **preparation**: you know your objective, what are your tactics? How are you going to make the most of your opportunity? What questions should you ask? Then, as the moment of the appointment approaches, how can you best prepare yourself physically (what should you wear?) and emotionally (what mood do you wish to evoke in yourself?) Afterwards, of course, you go back to your desk at home and get out your **log-book**. Now is the time to *review*. What were the key things that were said? What did you say you will do? How was *your* side of things? Could you do better next time? Should there be a 'next time' and if so why?

Other ways in which you can make the most of individuals to help you achieve your goal are two forms of **mental rehearsal**. You can identify the skills you most need to improve (**skills assessment** exercise), you can think of a person who performs one of the skills particularly well and construct a visualisation of him or her doing this skill – and then become that person in your visualisation (the **ideal model** visualisation). Alternatively you can wait until you actually have to perform that skill and act 'as if' you are that person, as you perform. In the first case the visualisation is done in your bedroom at home, in the second it is done in the place of your performance. (In both cases you are probably reowning a projection – or at least there will be some element of this in the exercise).

Summary
Goalsetting (p.36)
Preparation and review, (p.141)
Log-book (p.147)
Skills assessment exercise (pp.43-54)
Mental rehearsal (p.153)

Your team

If you are part of a synergistic team – the sort of team where the whole is greater than the sum of its parts – you have a powerful resource. Your interaction, contribution and place within the whole assures you access to the team's wisdom and strength. A synergistic team affirms the best in each individual member which in itself is a source of comfort and energy. A team is also a source of ideas and of a wide range of skills.

This is one of the best ways possible to ensure that you actualise your Vision and attain your objective. In such a team it is a given that the *team* Vision is one which includes all the individual team members being helped to reach and express their full potential. No one member is sacrificed for the others, for this would mean that the team is not performing perfectly. At the same time, from your point of view, you are supported in expressing yourself fully in a certain context and it is your willingness to play your part (to demonstrate your goodwill) that leads you forward.

Of course, not all teams have such high ideals and if you are a member of two or three different teams, in different contexts, you may need to look to your experience in the one which is closest to the ideal as being your greatest resource. Nevertheless the way that you choose to act as a team member in any team of which you are part will affect your performance and your progress towards achieving your goal.

Action

In any team, individual members should take responsibility for their own **preparation and review**, constructing their own ritual which they perform in order to be able to contribute fully to the team's performance. From there on the team is also your personal resource. A small group of team members or the team as a whole will attune to any obstacle that you encounter and brainstorm on ways in which it may be reduced or overcome.

To some extent your mental image of the team is itself a resource and this maybe reinforced by a **picture** – a team photograph – the team **song**, the team **slogan** or even the team trophy or **mascot**.

Summary
Preparation and review (p.141)
Picture (p.159)
Music (p.166)
Slogan (p.144)
Symbol (p.161)
Mascot (p.164)

Information

You might also need information to improve your performance. In our 'information age' there is a whole host of resources you might use in information centres, libraries, cassettes and video. Use them well. The process of research has its own rewards. And becoming an authority on a subject can offer detachment and a wider perspective.

Some very gifted athletes – particularly team athletes who are coached by an authoritarian coach – fail to think for themselves about their personal performance. This means that they do not improve and occasionally find themselves in a slump with little idea what it is they are doing differently. For them, getting information on their own initiative can be a rewarding process – and result in a better performance.

Action
Information gathering should be a part of your mental training. First work out where you can get the information you need or might one day need – from other **people** or from **books** – and then work out when and how to use the information you have in the course of doing your **preparation and review**.

Summary
Reading (p.148)
People (p.170)
Preparation and review (p.141)

Art

The experience and vision of others expressed in various art forms may evoke creativity, inspiration, moods and feelings which help you along your way. Novels, poetry, films, pictures, sculpture, music, dance, opera and theatre are all possible resources for you. Many sports people draw on art-related images to inspire their performance. Nearly all athletes with whom we work make some use at least of music and photography. Art has sustained mankind since history began. If you've been brought up to feel it's an indulgence or a waste of time, put this view to one side for a moment and give it a try. Many people find art can help to get things in perspective in troubled times.

If, unlike the intuitive football player at the mercy of a sudden slump, you have been trained to believe that statistics and analysis will meet all your mental training needs, you are just as prone to being stuck on a plateau of no improvement. You will not reach your potential unless you use both hemispheres of your brain.

Action

So having identified your **goal** and **assessed** your level of skill, draw up a plan of action which includes representation and evocation of the ideal that you seek, in not one but several different art forms. Imitate the young British team cyclists who have a space on their bedroom wall reserved for their current mental training **photograph** – the photo of someone or something that evokes their experience of the techniques or quality that they are currently aiming to improve. (The photo is changed each ten days or two weeks, as they change the skill on which they are working.)

Discover a poet with whom you can empathise and look through this work for a **poem** or a verse that captures your particular dream or reinforces the attitude you know you need to adopt to make your next step forward. When you find the poem, learn a few lines and perhaps write a couple out as you might an **affirmation**. Put the lines under your photograph, just for the period of time that you are working to improve that particular skill.

Take time off to arrange to visit an art gallery nearby. Draw on the peace or inner conflict of the artist. Give yourself the time to do this. You deserve it.

Having identified an obstacle on your path, look through the **music** tapes you have at home and find a track or a piece that mobilises your energy in exactly the right way for you to take up the challenge with confidence and enthusiasm. Or pull out all those old colour supplements still lurking in the kitchen or sitting room and make a **collage** to represent the way in which you will win that particular battle. The possibilities are endless.

Summary

Goalsetting (p.36)
Skills assessment exercise (pp.43-54)
Picture (p.159)
Collage (p.160)
Poetry (p.148)

Affirmation (p.142)
Music (p.161)

Self-improvement groups

Since the emergence of 'T' (for training) groups, the forerunner of Encounter group workshops, some 35 years ago, self-improvement groups have come of age. Early principles and exercises have been fused with the teachings and methods of the older humanistic psychologies – Gestalt and psycho-synthesis in particular – and rigorous new disciplines have emerged. Amongst these, Neurolinguistic Programming and Transactional Analysis have become widely used, if in simplified form, within the educational structure of large business corporations.

The advantage that a well-led self-improvement group has over any other type of team is that it will specifically support your process of change. Self-improvement groups are largely for those people who realise that they want to make such changes and so particular attention is given to building a climate for respect and trust at a very early stage. Other teams will support development and growth particularly in relation to team performance but a self-improvement group is constructed to support (sometimes total) change.

Don't be put off by the jargon or the names: Gestalt, psychosynthesis, NLP, TA, and Jungian dream groups all offer the creative environment and support of the best teams whilst being a particular insightful source of feedback. Depending on your needs and where you are at the moment, you might consider disciplines further from mainstream thought and codes of behaviour. Rogerian therapy, Reichian therapy, Janov groups and bioenergetics all offer valuable insight.

Action
If you are reading this book for ideas which may support a major change of direction in your life, rather than to go

further faster in a chosen direction, look out for a congenial but challenging group to join.

Having **read** available magazines, been to your local library, citizen's advice bureau or health food shop, where such groups are often advertised, and discovered an appropriate group, try it. When you realise you are already fully engaged in the process, develop new personal **rituals** to fix your emerging changed view of life, find **music**, new music for you, which evokes this new perspective, keep in touch with old **friends** or acquaintances (as well as new friends from the group) that support your process.

Summary
Reading (p.148)
Ritual (p.165)
Music (p.166)
People (p.170)

The environment

We have already mentioned your memory of various environments. You can also develop a 'library' of real places to go, according to the mood or atmosphere you need to experience. Make a list in your log-book of extremes that are available to you and under each heading write down the mood it inspires:

> somewhere dark/somewhere light
> somewhere enclosed/somewhere open
> somewhere empty/somewhere crowded (with furniture or people),
> somewhere private/somewhere public,
> somewhere cool/somewhere warm,
> somewhere familiar/somewhere strange,
> somewhere at home/somewhere abroad,
> somewhere indoors/somewhere outdoors,

in the house/in the garden,
in the town/in the country,
at work/at home,

Each place you choose should inspire a particular positive
mood.

Making such an inventory also helps you to recognise
different parts of yourself, each with its own set of needs.
When you ignore some part of yourself for too long, your
concentration will falter and you'll find yourself getting irritable
(or, if like us when writing, hungry!) Having become aware of
your different selves, or subpersonalities, you can draw on a
wider range of ability in your efforts to attain your goal.

Action
In order to use your 'library' of places to visit or create
effectively, you should first do the **skills assessment** exercise
to determine which aspects of your performance you need to
improve most. When you want to improve your endurance, you
think of the nearest agreeable place where you can go running.
If you need to improve your tennis serve or your ability to
bargain, what is the easiest, least distracting environment in
which you can practise? If you need to be more courageous
how can you change your room (or one room in your house)
so that it becomes a place that helps you to get in touch with
the feeling of courage? Or what place is there out of doors that
you can visit that gives you that feeling?

Note down in your log book when you become most cowardly
and when you find yourself to be naturally brave. What sort of
situations provoke each extreme? Is there any pattern? Do you
find yourself to be more courageous at the beginning or the end
of the day and how far does that depend on where you are? As
you experiment with the effects of different environments keep
a record of the results so that you can gradually build a support
system for yourself.

Eventually you will be able to evoke your courage or the

quality of performance you wish to develop, at will, by calling a particular environment to mind. This is the way the **Quiet Place** visualisation works, evoking the memory or creating the fantasy of a place that is peaceful and unthreatening for you. Developing such a place, doing the **Quiet Place** visualisation, is in fact a good exercise in any circumstances, since it becomes a tool which you can use at a moment's notice, whenever you need it. It also develops your consciousness of the component parts of an environment, especially those you experience other than visually.

Summary
Skills assessment exercise (p.43-54)
Log-book (p.147)
Quiet Place visualisation (p.156)

Objects

When you are trapped in a particular environment, in your bedroom, in hospital, in a hotel, or when you are working so hard that you see nothing but your place of work and your home, you still have a few resources, objects which in themselves create support for your performance or which can be made to do so by placing them in a certain position, relative to the room, to yourself or, in the case of more than one object, to each other. Objects, like the various forms of art, are themselves listed by us as mental training exercises.

Action
'These foolish things' can all inspire feelings and moods that you need to experience at certain times. Plants, shrubs and trees, flowers and fruit may all be right at specific times. To capitalise on these, you need to compose your library, for future reference.

Again it is necessary to begin with a **goalsetting** exercise and a **skills assessment** exercise to establish your direction and objective. Then you look around for objects which will reinforce whatever aspect of your performance it is that needs to be strengthened.

Used in this way, objects become **symbols**. They are invested with power and meaning by you or by the team of which you are a part. The conch shell was invested with authority by the children in William Golding's *Lord of the Flies*: as they developed a ritual of 'council meetings', the conch became the symbol of the power to speak whilst everyone else listened. He who held the conch held sway. In the same way, you could invest an object that is given to you by a friend with the dominant positive quality that you perceive in that friend. A stone that you found on a deserted beach last summer can be given the power to evoke the feeling of strength and happiness that you experienced there. It actually becomes a touchstone.

As with all your resources, it is conscious intention and planned regular usage which can transform any object into a mental training exercise.

Summary
Goalsetting (p.36)
Skills assessment exercise (p.43-54)
Symbol (p.161)

9

Preparation
for performance

If you have worked systematically through this book, you will now have filled much of your log book. At the beginning there will be your vision and your prioritised goals. This will be followed by a record of your strengths and weaknesses, in terms of current physical, technical and mental skill. Next you will have a detailed record of the obstacles you identified as being in your path, the resources you have at your disposal and a detailed list of mental training exercises that will lead you past these obstacles towards your particular goal.

The final step is to organise your observations and your lists of mental training exercises into an effective mental training programme . . . well, the penultimate step anyway: the final step is to put that programme into operation!

To take this step, we should first clarify the scope of such a programme and then look at the relationship of mental training to mental preparation. This will allow us to correct two common misunderstandings about thinking to win – the first being that mental training means training the mind rather than using the mind (it doesn't) and the second being that mental preparation and mental training mean the same thing (they don't). This chapter is therefore divided into three parts.

- Mental training vs. mental skills

- Mental preparation vs. mental training
- Building your mental training programme.

Part one: Mental skills vs. mental training

Many coaches believe mental training exercises are designed only to improve mental skills. The coach who thinks this way will consider calling us in because an athlete has a problem with concentration or the whole squad seems to be low on confidence. Of course we can help because mental training *does* improve mental skills but it is designed to improve physical and technical skills as well. We have to explain to coaches that we see it as much their responsibility to focus on and improve mental skills in their technical training sessions as it is for us to use our mental training sessions to improve physical and technical skills through exercises such as, for instance, goal-setting and visualisation.

One of the exercises we give coaches, when we are invited to run an advanced Sporting Bodymind workshop, is to brainstorm on how they would devise a normal (technical) training session to develop concentration, patience, confidence, the ability to deal with stress, and so on. We divide them into small groups and get each group to brainstorm on developing a particular mental skill.

The three types of training form a matrix with the three types of skill. Each trainer, physical, technical and mental, is going to affect all three skills anyway, according to the content and manner of the presentation. We call out consultancy Sporting Bodymind to emphasise that anything good or bad that affects the body will also affect the mind and vice versa. So why not do it consciously? Why should physical trainers assume they only have a responsibility for developing physical skills? Why should the coaches, the technical trainers, assume that they only have a responsibility to develop technical skills? It's because they do that they assume the mental trainer only has the responsibility to develop mental skills.

The training matrix

	Physical Skills	Technical Skills	Mental Skills
Physical Training	1	2	3
Technical Training	4	5	6
Mental Training	7	8	9

This is not the place to go into great detail, largely because the technical skills can vary so much in every field. However, whatever your Vision, your way towards it involves your physical, technical and mental presence; and the state of your physical being is going to affect your performance as much as the state of your mind. Sports people are perhaps one step ahead of others in realising this. So let's look at the matrix for just a moment and give a couple of examples.

Physical trainers and teachers of any discipline promoting physical health are comfortable in box 1. Sports coaches, technical training staff or teachers of anything from plastering to dance are comfortable in box 5. We as mental trainers are comfortable in boxes 7, 8 and 9. For you to get a complete training, your physical trainer or health instructor must be imaginative and consider boxes 2 and 3, your coach or technical trainer must use his or her imagination and consider boxes 4 and 6.

Trainers need to adjust their training to develop all skills. Thus considering box 3, physical trainers might develop concentration, a mental skill, by organising their sequences of exercises in a complicated way, or they might develop the ability of their trainees to deal with stress by carefully introducing bursts of very high work load in stamina training. Considering box 6, technical trainers, might develop concentration by providing deliberate distractions during their coaching session or technical training programme. If they want to develop patience, they could ask their athletes or trainers to stick at a particular exercise for much longer than normal (without declaring their intention until later).

The exercises you've been building into your mental training programme can be entered in boxes 7, 8 and 9. For example, **Visualisation** may be used to develop strength, a badminton service or aggression or (in the context of business) it can develop the ability to relax, the ability to sell or confidence – in each case, physical, technical and mental skills.

Part two: Mental preparation vs. mental training

Now let's look at the second common misunderstanding: that mental preparation is synonymous with mental training. We define mental training as using your mind to improve your performance and this can (and should) be done during and after your performance as well as before. Of course, mental training is also preparation in the sense that all training is preparation – physical and technical training as well. Top athletes, like the top pianists, train every day not just to prepare for the big event but to maintain, explore and expand their ability. And serious training includes a physical, technical and mental component.

Mental training should be used to perfect your preparation routine as well as to perfect your performance. The way in which you prepare should be as clear in your mind as your actual performance, otherwise your performance itself will be below par. Your preparation routine should be designed to bring you to a point of physical, emotional and mental readiness. If you haven't discovered how to do this, no matter how clear your intended performance may be in your mind, no matter how many times you have rehearsed it, it will not be right.

Prior to the 1990 Junior World Cycling Championships, I had seven days to introduce the basic mental training to the British team pursuit team and reached a stage where the four young riders were communicating openly and could visualise their intended ride well. Unfortunately, I left no time to work on their preparation routine. In the event, the hour preceding their ride was chaotic, as each rider adopted his own habitual routine but lost touch with each of the others. They rode very fast and were heading for a record time but the ride was untidy and, three laps from the end, one rider touched the wheel of the rider in front one time too many and crashed. Afterwards I had to point out that their own dejected description of the ride as 'ragged' and 'all over the place' was a precise description of their unrehearsed preparation routine. It was a valuable lesson for us all.

Preparation itself can be divided into three overlapping parts: long term preparation, preparation on the day, and preparation at intervals throughout your performance.

Long term preparation

Paradoxically, the clearer you are on your ideal preparation routine, the better you are able with unexpected circumstances prior to your performance. The junior cyclists were not clear about preparation and were further distracted by intensely hot weather and a delay in the programme. The Preview-Review exercise on page 141 asks you to consider the three aspects to long-term as well as to more immediate preparation – physical, emotional and mental.

Mental preparation should normally be completed before you focus on emotional or physical preparation. Mental preparation, as contrasted with emotional and physical preparation, involves setting goals for the performance and deciding how you are going to achieve them. Team sports people don't often do this, confusing the team goals and tactics with a standard they might set for themselves and a plan as to how they personally will contribute to the team achieving its goal. If we ask such a player what his or her objective is prior to a match, we'll get the reply 'To win, of course' which quite misses the point. 'So what are *you* going to do to help the team win?' we then ask.

First establish your goals and your plan of action, preferably a day or two in advance, and write it down in your log book, so that you may refer to it afterwards. Then see how well you did and set more appropriate goals or tactics for next time.

Some emotional and physical preparation should also be done in advance of the day of performance. Emotional preparation is anything which ensures you are in the right mood to perform. If you know that over the last three performances you've started nervously and off-key, then you may begin preparing for this performance a week beforehand, by developing and using an **affirmation** and a **mental rehearsal** or by focusing on some piece of calm **music** or on a colleague or **friend** whom you think to be calm.

Physical preparation might be making some change in your normal diet, going to bed earlier than usual, checking any special equipment or clothing you'll need, or – if you're an athlete and injured – getting appropriate treatment from your physiotherapist.

Preparation on the day

Preparation on the day, at the place where you're going to perform is what the athlete calls 'warming-up' and we call 'attunement'. 'Attunement' or 'tuning in' to something means focusing one's attention on it. We identify seven objects of attunement, all of which have to be gone through by the athlete, for he or she to be quite ready. The same process applies to a business meeting, a class, or the start of a day at the computer, or a personal discussion, even though on many occasions, your warm-up can be brief. The point is that if you don't warm-up and attune to these various factors in turn, you may find yourself unprepared and distracted by one or more of them after your performance has begun.

The place

The first factor is the place of performance itself. If you're leading a meeting, check the meeting room. Although there may be no full ashtrays and empty coffee cups from the last people using it, the arrangement of chairs and tables may not suit your purpose. If you're having a brainstorming session you'll want the chairs in a circle and the tables out of the way. If you're giving a talk to a large group of visitors, you may decide to put the chairs in rows facing one end of the room. You might also decide to put signs outside to show where the room is and have a 'meeting in progress' sign ready to put on the door when you start.

Such actions are the *result* of tuning into the place, when first you arrive. Get a sense of the atmosphere too, 'make friends' with it by finding something familiar that you like about it, so that you can begin to feel that it is *your* territory, that you are at home there. Before the FA Cup Final in London there is a tradition that each team in turn walks out on to the Wembley pitch. We've done this twice with Tottenham, all of us dressed in identical, especially tailored suits. The noise of the 100,000 flag-waving spectators is extraordinary. The atmosphere unique. Yet the ritual serves a valuable purpose. It allows the players to tune in to the excitement and to examine the state of the pitch. When it's time to come through the tunnel for the opening ceremony and the start of the match, both teams have an idea of what to expect.

If you are at home, preparing for another day's work at your computer, the parallel may be hard to find. Yet it is there. How do you like the temperature? How much air is there in the room? Is the answer machine on, if you don't want to be disturbed? Can you work comfortably in a room that's disordered? Do you want the dogs in or out? Whatever your performance and wherever you perform take time to check in to the place where you are. If there's something that needs changing, change it. If you can't, then find a way to change your response.

Yourself

Changing your response involves tuning into yourself, realising that you can be in charge, that your feelings are not necessarily governed by your surroundings. In fact, having tuned into your surroundings, it's important to tune into how you feel – both emotionally and physically – and what thoughts there are knocking about in your head.

If you're not ready physically for your performance, what is it you need to do? Athletes have to stretch and exercise their muscles or have a massage. You may need a glass of water, to visit the lavatory or to open a new packet of Kleenex tissues. You may want to comb your hair, take off your jacket or crack your finger joints. Do whatever makes you feel ready to go – either now or a short time later.

If your head is full of distracting thoughts – an argument you had last night, a relative who is ill, an interview you have to attend in a couple of days time – or if you feel out of it emotionally or are distracted by something in the environment that is not pertinent to your performance, either write these things down on a piece of paper and put in a pocket where you'll find it later or, better still, do the **Black Box** visualisation as (p.155). Very often just taking a moment of silence, allows you to recognise that you are still in a rush, that your body has arrived but your mind has not. Give yourself this time.

If you are upset by something in the environment that is not pertinent to your performance, seek some wider perspective – perhaps it's there for the benefit of someone else who in an expanded sense is part of the same team as yourself, and at this level has similar objectives. Alternately ask yourself 'What could I *gain* from this apparent distraction?'

Equipment

You will have made sure that you have all the equipment you need and that it's in good order, during the first phase of preparations but if you use a hammer, a fountain pen, a stop watch or a forklift truck, take a moment to give it your full attention before you begin. Say 'hello!' to it, if you like. It may even help if you give it a name, as some golfers do their clubs. That moment before Stefan Edberg leaves his chair and bangs one racket against another and, having made his selection, bangs it against the heel of his hand is an important part of his attunement.

Other people

If you are going to perform with other people, whether or not they have a similar role, you'll perform better if you first tune into them. If you arrive late, give yourself at least a moment to go through the first three steps of attunement before launching into animated conversation. Apart from anything else, in many situations, the latecomer who speaks before picking up the threads and tuning in is resented. But, having tuned in to your surroundings, yourself and your equipment, you may give your full attention to others.

You may need to check out technical or tactical information or you may just stand there with a cup of coffee, discussing the vagaries of the weather, but beyond this you are becoming aware of each person, making contact so that you'll play instinctively to each other's strengths as soon as the performance begins. Whether or not you then tune into an opponent you have is a matter of personal taste. In the sports world there are many who make a point of ignoring their opponents until the last minute but in another situation, such as an interview where your interviewers could be said to be pitting themselves against you, it may be to your advantage to turn your attention towards them.

The team

This step may not apply to your situation but, if you are performing as a member of a team, it's important to attune to the team as a whole, becoming aware again of what it feels like when you create something together which, as a mere collection of individuals you'd be unable to do. If you are part of a synergistic team there will be a host of norms and rituals which will make this process relatively easy. If you are distracted by some unpleasant recent memory, look around and recall prior excitements when, together with these people, you have performed well.

Your purpose

Even if you've been immersed in the same job for three weeks, take a moment each morning to get a wider perspective and attune to your particular goal. You decided this, perhaps long ago, in the first phase of preparation but now, before picking up where you left off last night, tune into it again. If you're writing a report, make a one sentence statement of its message. Think again for a moment about who it is for. If you're going to give a speech or preach a sermon, do the same. If you're about to go on stage, think about your connection with the audience. If you're part of team, tune into your personal goal, your own task, and review how it contributes to the objective of the team as a whole.

The activity

Now bring your attention back to how you are going to achieve that purpose – how you intend to begin your performance, what stages it will go through and what gambits, if any, you'll employ. The professional or national sports team's version of attuning to purpose and activity is the pre-match peptalk in which, having invoked team spirit, the coach reminds the players of the goals and tactics that were either announced or agreed upon earlier in the week.

For you, in terms of beginning a day's work and having tuned in to your objective, tuning in to the activity means getting clear how you will organise your day. Tackling a personal problem might mean running over in your mind what you are going to say, how you might respond, and what the options are.

Preparation at intervals during your performance

Sports people often fail because of lapses of concentration. The cricketer gets out or is hit for six; the tennis player loses a critical point. We usually find that these athletes have no clear idea *how* they prepare to receive, bowl or serve and are therefore unable to ensure that they prepare properly: they are easily distracted.

If your own performance is one which is broken up into a series of actions or new starts and you find that on your **skills assessment** exercise your figure against concentration was high, you may also need to establish a routine for preparation. This could be valuable for a situation like passing a driving test, where you must recover from successful or unsuccessful negotiation of one element and prepare to put your full attention on the next, or for you as an interviewer who find your attention wandering already after talking to the third applicant. Such a routine would even help you to learn to restrain a fiery temper at appropriate moments: if you establish an attentional routine, you can choose to use it when you feel your anger rising.

The attentional routine to go through as a way of preparation, has to be based on a past experience. Ideally it is an experience where you concentrated and performed well first but, if you can't recall such an occasion, it will be one where you blew it. In this case you begin changing elements of the previous build-up till, by trial and error, you come up with a routine that works.

There are two exercises that help to introduce and explain the nature of an attentional routine. The first is a Gestalt exercise called 'Hello-Goodbye'. For this you need to find a colleague or a friend, sit opposite him or her and talk about anything that comes into your head. Allow this to develop into a conversation but, as soon as you feel your mind begin to wander or the slightest bit bored, say 'Goodbye', sit back in your chair and close your eyes.

When your eyes are closed, pay attention to the thoughts and feelings that were beginning to stir. After a while become aware of how it feels to sit there on the chair, which muscles are working and which are relaxed, right the way down from your head to your feet. Pay some attention to your breathing too.

In the meantime your colleague is quiet. Then, when you find your attention moving outside yourself wondering what's happening out there, what your partner is doing or thinking, open your eyes again, look at him or her and start another conversation by expressing whatever is in your mind.

After a while, you'll catch your mind wandering again. Then say 'Goodbye', maybe even in mid-sentence – a sentence that *either* of you were speaking – close your eyes and discover what's going on *inside* you. Continue in this way for ten minutes. Then write down what you have discovered. Perhaps after that your colleague would like to have a go.

The second exercise is one we've developed from psycho-synthesis. We call it '**Now I am aware**'. Again you need a colleague or friend to sit opposite you. The exercise is in two parts. In the first, you tell your colleague something of which you are aware that you can see straight in front of you and then something of which you are aware that you can see out of the corner of your eyes, as you continue to look straight ahead. Each statement must begin with the words 'Now I am aware . . .' and each statement should be immediately followed by another, alternately referring to something in front of you and something to one side. Your colleague says nothing at all, unless you go off into a dream or get stuck. He or she then prompts you by saying 'Now I am aware . . .?' After five minutes he tells you to stop.

The second part of the exercise is a little similar to **Hello-Goodbye**, in that here you speak first of something of which you're aware 'outside' you and then of something of which you're aware 'inside' you. The things outside you may be people, things or events, including sounds. The things inside you may be thoughts (including fantasies and memories), emotions, and physical sensations (including the kinaesthetic sense and the sense of touch) So, a typical sequence might be 'Now I am aware that you're looking at me', 'Now I am aware of an itch on my cheek', 'Now I am aware of the window behind you', 'Now I'm aware of feeling silly', 'Now I'm aware of the piano being played next door', 'Now I'm aware of the weight of my right leg on my left', 'Now I'm aware of the yellow carpet', 'Now I'm aware of wondering when the five minutes will be up', and so on.

On this occasion, unlike the 'Hello-Goodbye' exercise, you don't close your eyes to consult what's happening inside, unless at first it is difficult for you without doing so. Again you must follow one sentence with the next and your colleague prompts you with 'Now I am aware . . .?' if you get stuck. After five minutes he or she tells you to stop and you can either write down or discuss what you discovered as you did the exercise.

Both these exercises help to stop your attention from going into the Middle Zone, the obstacle we described in Chapter 5. You are in the Middle Zone when you talk or listen distractedly to someone whilst worrying about something that is happening somewhere else. In fact, your attention is rapidly flitting from outside to inside and back, never giving you enough time to focus properly. It is this type of distractedness to which a sports person often refers, coming to us with the complaint that he or she spaces out at unpredictable or important moments. If your concentration lapses during your driving test, it could well be because your attention is rapidly shifting from the road out there to wondering whether you did well enough on the three-point turn.

Robert Nideffer's concept of attention being either broad or narrow, internal or external has had its detractors but still serves as a useful model in the context of 'preparation at intervals during your performance', – especially if you are concerned to maintain perfect concentration throughout. According to this model there are four classes of attentional focus: broad internal, narrow internal, broad external and narrow external. Perceptions of your inner and outer world may be grouped under these headings as in the following table:

	Broad	*Narrow*
Internal	*thoughts feelings*	*physical sensations*
External	*people, things and events happening peripherally or on a broad scope*	*people, things and events happening straight ahead or on a narrow scope*

The table can be used to identify possible focii of attention in a given situation. When we worked with a tennis player who said he spaced out when serving at crucial moments, we asked him to remember first a game in which he served well and then a game in which he served poorly and in each case to think back and make a list of the things of which he was aware and in what order. We asked him to reflect on the differences and talk about them and then see if he could think of any improvement in the routine that he'd had on the occasion he served well. (Had he not been able to, that would have been okay).

Since he had trouble remembering where his attention was focused and how it changed, we explained the four categories and went through each in turn. 'What are the things outside you, of which you need to be aware? Is there a moment before serving when you like to take in the whole court or the atmosphere of the place? What are the specific people, things or events on which you need to focus? Perhaps the umpire, a friend or your coach, probably the ball and and your opponent, or perhaps something I'd never think of like the ring on your finger, the service line, or the seam on the ball?'

Then we asked about things happening 'inside' himself. 'What thoughts do you like to have?' 'Do you repeat an affirmation? Review your goal or your tactics? Run through an instant pre-play visualisation of the ball you're about to serve?' Then 'What mood do you like to be in? How can you instantly create that mood? Where in your body do you seem to experience it? How exactly do you feel physically when you have that mood? What happens?'

Finally we moved to the internal narrow category (without naming it) and asked him about his kinaesthetic sensations and his sense of touch. 'Do you like to be aware of how your weight is distributed at any point prior to serving? If you bounce the ball, how many times are you aware of the movement of your arm and wrist or the contact between the ball and your hand? Do you at any point like to be aware of the weight of your racket head and your grip on the handle?'

He didn't know the answers to all these questions but he was able to find out and, by a process of trial and error, he could discover not only where he needed to put his attention but also *when*, so that he finished up with what we've been calling an attentional routine. Of course there is no right answer. Two different players will invariably have different routines but, once discovered, their personal routine becomes an essential element of their preparation. Could your performance be more consistent? If so, think about the attendance routine you adopt when performing well.

Knowing when to withdraw attention from what's happening outside, like stepping back to the position of an observer to assess your performance and how far you are towards reaching your goal, allows for maximum effort when you return into the fray. In terms of concentration, only yogis or mystics can hold their attention on one thing for more than a few seconds. (Try it.) But by making a switch from outside to inside and from narrow to broad, as your performance allows, helps you to be fully present and prepared for long periods of time.

Part three: Building your mental training programme

Building your mental training programme is a major move towards realising your new Vision. Set aside a couple of hours at a time of day when you are feeling alert and ready to move on. Begin by warming-up in the sequence we've just described and then take these further steps in turn.

- Tune in to your Vision
  For some time now you have been engrossed in details. Building them into an apt and coherent programme requires a clear sense of your goal. Take a moment to review those first pages of your log book and re-experience the clarity and excitement of your Vision.

- Review your prioritised goals
  These are the stages along the path towards realising your Vision. Gradually focus your attention on attaining the first of these goals.

- Review the details of where you are now
  Check the results of your skills assessment exercise. Which skills are those that most need improvement? Look over the obstacles and resources that you have identified – both those that are inside yourself and those that are outside. Re-read the lists of mental training exercises that follow each obstacle and resource.

- Tune in to the 'Big Picture'
  Now retreat again from the detail without losing sight of it: look at the situation as if through the other end of a telescope. What stands out over all? What is the 'big picture'? There will be repetition, overlapping and reinforcement. There will be a pattern. What is the dominant shape? What is the headline of the overall message? If this is where you are (in terms of skills,

obstacles and resources) and that is your first objective, what is the obvious step to take? What is it that clearly needs doing and where should you begin right now?

- Make these first steps the focus of your mental training programme and then identify practical details.
A mental training programme is a list of decisions, headed by one-off actions that precede the chosen mental training exercises. For instance, if you've been browsing through this book and only now decide to follow it in detail, your first action would be to buy a log book in which to record your training. Action often begins by talking to someone, proclaiming your intention to your family, your teacher or your coach. Perhaps you need to make some kind of a booking by telephone or arrange a meeting with a friend. If you have an office, you may start by rearranging the furniture. If your Vision is closely related to home life, you may need to clean out the content of drawers or get an estimate on the cost of having the roof fixed. Decide this one-off action first.

- Write down these one-off decisions
Your mental training programme requires a new section of your log-book. We suggest the heading 'Mental Training Programme' and the date. Then the word 'objective' underlined and a description of this your first step. Beneath that again write the heading 'One-off actions' and list the decisions you have just made. Each decision should have time by which the action will be completed, if possible exactly when it will be done and, if it isn't obvious, where it will be done. Beneath this list leave a space and then write the heading 'On-going actions'.

- Review your resources
Which of your resources did you identify as being most related to achieving your original goals? Which is the

resource that can most help you to achieve this first step? How can you best use it? and how might you reinforce that resource? Decide what you will do to utilise and reinforce that resource and put this at the head of your list of 'on-going actions'.

● Select the appropriate mental training exercises
A comprehensive range of our mental training exercises are described in the next chapter. Many of them, such as visualisation, affirmations and music, can be used to reach any objective. For instance, if you look back at the Skills Assessment exercise and the skill which you feel you most need to develop at the moment, you will find that you can do this through a wide variety of these exercises.

However, the task here is to settle on a few mental training exercises which will help you to make the 'first step', that became clear as you contemplated the 'big picture'. These exercises may be those suggested in relation to the resources and obstacles you've identified on your route – your 'first step' may have been to tackle a particular obstacle or reinforce a particular resource – but your 'big picture' may also have suggested another starting point around which to build your programme. In this case you will find that as you focus on that objective, having read through the book so far, you will know which exercises to choose. The choosing process will be easier as you realise the wide scope and applicability of all the exercises and the fact that none can do harm. At worst you will learn through trial and error.

Start with the most general and choose at least one exercise that involves thinking *about* your performance (a left-brain exercise, such as **morning planning**, **evening review**, an **affirmation**) and one exercise that involves thinking *of* your performance (a right-brain exercise, such as **visualisation**, the use of **music** or **drawing**).

- Look up your chosen exercises in the next chapter and try them out
A full account of all the exercises is given in Chapter 10. Look up the ones you have chosen and read them through. Then give each exercise a try, noting how long each one takes and its degree of difficulty for you.

- Decide the time you have available per day for mental training and reduce your programme if necessary
Most of the mental training exercises should be practised for a period of time each day. A relaxation exercise and a mental rehearsal should take at least five minutes, probably ten. An evening review will take as long. It is easy to overcommit yourself and better to set a simple target at first. Mental training needs to be practised as regularly as any other form of serious training, if you want to achieve your goal. Decide now which exercises you will keep, how long you will devote to them, how often, at what time of day, where and for how many days. A mental training programme will usually need adjusting or replacing – a new programme for the next step along the way – every ten days or two weeks.

- Write out the finalised programme in your log book
Rewrite the programme, with its duration and starting date clearly marked. Record your progress day by day, if only by a series of ticks. You may have a teammate, colleague or friend who is beginning mental training with you but this is essentially a personal process and demands considerable discipline. If your targets are correct you will find it easier to maintain momentum as you begin to see results. These results also need to be recorded.

- Repeat the cycle
When your first programme is finished, go back to the beginning, tune in to your Vision once more and discover

your next step. This might be improving a skill, tackling an obstacle, reinforcing a strength or, once again, a step that emerges from each of these that you see clearly as you look at the 'big picture'. Then, consulting Chapter 10 once more, build yourself a new mental training programme.

10

Mental training exercises

Here is a full account of each of the mental training exercises, many of which have been mentioned in earlier chapters. They are here for reference, as and when you need them but it would probably help to read the chapter through before you set up your first mental training programme.

We divide the exercises into those which involve *thinking about* your performance – the left-brain analytical exercises – and those which involve *thinking* of your performance – the right brain associative ones. We'll look at the analytical exercises first. (Such exercises include the **goalsetting** and **skills assessment** we went through together at the beginning of this book).

1 Thinking about your performance: analytical exercises

Preview – Review

This exercise is designed to guide you towards establishing a pre-performance and post-performance routine that ensures correct preparation and a valuable review. Start by choosing a specific past performance, good or bad, triumph or disaster, that was important to you and that you can remember well. Then make a list of all the things you did to prepare for that event, dividing them into those things which helped you be mentally prepared (that helped you to know what you were going to do and how you were going to do it) those things that helped you to be emotionally prepared (that made you feel in the right mood) and those things which helped you to be physically prepared.

Then note down which of these preparations was the most important before making a new list, this time of all the other things you can think of now, either mental, emotional or physical, that you might also have done to prepare but didn't. When you've done that give yourself a score out of ten for how well you prepared for that performance.

On another sheet make a similar list of what you did after the performance was over. How did you warm down physically? – Did you wash? have coffee? eat? rest? sleep? stretch? go to the lavatory? go for a walk?

How did you warm down emotionally, getting back to 'neutral' after the excitement of 'winning' or the frustration of 'losing'? And how did you warm down mentally? Did you review the result in the light of your original objectives and did you review your tactics?

Once all this is done you again pick out the factor in your actual review that you think was the best and then make a new list of all the other things – physical, emotional, or mental – that you now realise you might have done to review better. When you've done this score yourself out of ten for how well you reviewed and reflect on the exercise as a whole. If you were from now on to adopt a basic preparation and review routine what should they be?

Affirmation

An affirmation is a positive sentence that is derived from a description you make of a past positive performance. It usually refers to some specific aspect of that performance, a particular skill – physical, technical or mental – that you performed perfectly or better than ever before. The affirmation is a way of keeping that memory alive and present, overlaying more recent memories of times when you performed the skill less well.

When retrieving the memory and discovering the affirmation initially, it is best to be sitting down and relaxed. You may close your eyes and visualise the event (see **Visualisation** p.150) or you may be describing the event to a colleague or team mate who notes down any part of your description that describes how you *feel* as you perform that way. The vividly recalled memory is bound to have a strong kinaesthetic component if the situation involved movement. Even if it doesn't, you should notice the posture you are in and how you feel physically as well as emotionally.

If you are alone and want to get such an affirmation, you could use a cassette recorder. Sit back and play the memory through once to yourself and then play it through again and describe what you experience – what you see, hear, do and above all what you feel as you perform this skill so well.

Having done this, look over the notes your colleague has taken or play back the recording you've made and pick out the words or full sentence that best describes how it felt to perform that way. Then form those words or change the sentence into a short sentence which begins with the word 'I' and continues in the present tense. This is your affirmation. You don't have to repeat it to yourself. It is better to put it somewhere where you'll see it several times a day and to leave it there for a ten-day or two-week period only, whilst you work through a programme of other mental, technical and perhaps physical training exercises to improve that particular skill.

Here are some examples of affirmations:

A first division football player we worked with whose objective was to regain his ability to score goals, mentally rehearsed the last perfect goal he had scored and got the affirmation 'I hit it sweet.'

A jazz pianist who recognised that his lack of confidence and habitual pessimism had distanced him from the rest of the band he had recently joined and was affecting the entire performance, mentally rehearsed the delight he had felt playing with his college friends and came up with the affirmation 'I expect the highest and the best!'

A chief executive who had already suffered a minor heart attack and was determined to slow down and spend more time with his family, gave a long description of how he imagined things could be and got the affirmation 'I have enough time, energy and resources.' All three found they'd moved a great pace towards their objective within a month (the footballer scored a goal one week later).

Mottos and slogans

Mottos and slogans are also sentences, usually shorter than an affirmation and not usually including the word 'I'. They either contain a simple technical message or are a verbal expression of your Vision. They can express a Vision that you share with the rest of your family (a family motto) or a Vision that you share with a team to which you belong. A team slogan will improve your performance as a member of that particular team only. It may reinforce your sense of belonging.

You may of course devise a private slogan for yourself. Again it will differ from an affirmation, in that it won't usually begin with the word 'I' and it is something you may retain for years rather than a few days. However, if it is to be of positive value for a long time, without trapping you in a past phase of development, you should make sure that it relates to your Vision.

To get your slogan, sit back in your chair, allow yourself to relax and go back to the experience of your Vision. Then ask yourself 'What's happening here?' 'What's the big picture?' and allow a simple expressive sentence that captures the experience to come to mind. A client who had acting ambitions and a Vision of calm confidence on the stage, found her slogan to be 'courage is from the heart'.

Evocative words

Evocative words may either be related to a specific type of performance or they may become part of your everyday vocabulary. Our usual example of the first type is John Maclean, as coach of Llanelli Rugby Football Club, discovering that when he shouted *Drive!* instead of *Push!* to his side during a match, the scrum pushed harder.

Evocative words which you might usefully bring into your vocabulary on a permanent basis are 'challenge' rather than 'difficult', 'trust' rather than 'hope', 'when' instead of 'if' and *'won't'* instead of 'can't' (as in 'I won't . . .' instead of 'I can't . . .').

Each of these changes brings energy into the particular situation in which they are used. This is the determining nature of an evocative word. See what others you can find.

Analytical problem solving

Problem solving helps create change. There are many different analytical methods and techniques promoted for problem solving but in most cases the methodology will first focus on identifying the problem and getting to 'root cause'. This should then be followed by decision analysis in which you assess various solutions to the problem and decide on the most appropriate. This in turn is followed by action planning or project management in which you establish a course of action for implementing your decision. The final stage is problem prevention. Here you consider all the possible things which might go wrong in your implementation and establish preventive action to avoid them or protective actions to deal with them should they still go wrong. There may be yet another stage after the implementation of your actions which examines

the whole process which contributed to the problem to begin
with leading to recommendations for changing the system but
this is most often concerned with organisations in which you
might be working.

On the simplest level, problem solving is about discovering
where you are, deciding where you want to go, identifying
what obstructs you from your objective and implementing
plans to overcome the obstacles and achieve your goals. The
main mistake when problem solving lies in either focussing too
much on the detail or spending too much time fantasising about
the future. In the first instance you may go to great lengths
analysing, differentiating, prioritising and planning only to
find out that when you actually achieve your goal it doesn't
really meet your original objectives or satisfy your Vision: the
future you create is not the one you want to live in! In the second
instance you may have great visions for the future and know
exactly how you will spend all the money or what you will say
when you accept the gold medal, but because you missed out on
all the planning and preparation, your fantasised future never
arrives.

It is important, therefore, in working with problems to have
'bifocal Vision'. You need continually to reference both levels
of awareness – Vision and aspiration – to assure that all your
planning will achieve the desired outcome and the analytical
planning processes to assure that you will actualise your Vision.
The earlier chapters in this book detailed an approach which
integrates both levels. In order to practise 'bifocal Vision' you
must continually ask two questions: 'What needs to happen
here and now?' and 'What needs to emerge or unfold?'

Whichever problem-solving process you use, watch for the
level of change it attempts to achieve. Does it deal with
massive amounts of information? Does it require you to
fill in a multitude of forms? Is it completely verbal? Is the
process fixed? If so take care – it's probably very systematic,
very rational, very linear and good only for problems which
are systematic, linear and rational. It will be effective for

mechanical problems but may not be for problems involving people.

Writing

Personal journal

There is a Gestalt principal which says, 'Express what you impress' or, 'Do unto others what you do to yourself.' This advice is aimed primarily at people who retroflect (who turn their criticism back on to themselves) but is also good for someone struggling to find the answer to a divergent problem (a personal or relationship problem which has no one answer). A journal is another way for you to gain distance from your performance, to step out of the daily whirl and become the observer.

Keeping a journal is a form of meditation and can be a calming exercise to do at night or centring exercise to do in the early morning. Although you may start each entry with a note of the date, this is not a diary which has to be filled in each day. There may be times when you write a page both morning and evening. There may be weeks or even months when you write nothing at all. If you decide to keep a journal, choose a book that you like, probably a book that is bound rather than the spiral or loose leaf type.

Log-book

This exercise you know! We described its importance at the beginning of the book.

Free writing

It could be argued that 'Free writing' and poetry (see below), despite being thoughts that are expressed in words, are ways of *thinking of* rather than thinking about your performance.

Free writing is another exercise to be used when you have a divergent problem to solve. It was described by Peter Elbow in his book *Writing without Teachers* as a way of overcoming a writer's block. For this you need an egg timer, sheets of A4 paper and your pen. Turn the egg timer so the sand begins to run through the glass and start to write, initially about your problem but with no pause at all for thought, for reading over what you've written, nor even for checking spelling, grammar or that you've dotted your Is and crossed your Ts.

When the sand has run through, stop and read through what you've written. Ninety per cent of it will be rubbish, of no use at all, but usually somewhere is at least the germ of an exciting new idea. Dig this out and elaborate, perhaps brainstorming with a friend.

Poetry
Poetry is a way of capturing feelings or insights about a certain theme, that exist on the periphery of your consciousness. The imposed structure of the poem obliges your mind to let go of a straightforward habitual approach and grasp at any string of words that are still vaguely related and fit in. You don't need to think of yourself as a poet. You can continue to take pride in your scientific or down-to-earth outlook on life. You have many important insights and ideas – perhaps more than most – that float around just outside your sphere of conscious attention. These insights have been created by your own unique life experience. Allow yourself to use this exercise at an appropriate moment and you will be surprised at the result.

Reading

Articles and books
Technical articles and books on the subject of your performance are an obvious source of valuable information. Certain obstacles may be overcome by reading alone. Certain articles and books will reinforce your existing strengths.

Some people we work with have to discipline themselves to read at all. They did enough enforced reading at school and now prefer to gain any information they need by the spoken word. The drawback of course is that there may be no one in the vicinity who has the information they need, (there may not even be anybody to point out that they need the information.) Be critical of yourself for a moment. How far do you rely on your coach, your friends, immediate superiors or family to give you the information you need to reach your potential? Are you in danger of not thinking for yourself any more? If so, what is the easiest form of written information about your field for you to obtain, read and digest on a regular basis for a month or two? Or if you are blocked by a particular obstacle, who do you know who might guide you to find some interesting article or chapter that could give you background information and new ideas?

Other people we work with have to discipline themselves to *stop* reading. Their problem is not that they don't read enough but that they read indiscriminately. If they have a newspaper they'll read it from front to back, and not just the headlines. If they have a three-hour train ride, they'll take books to consult, but buy magazines that catch their eye at the station bookstall and reach their destination without opening their briefcase. They'll pick the right reference book but forget to use the index because the first chapter looks so interesting.

This is all fine if your need is rest and withdrawal. It also has to be admitted that unexpectedly useful ideas and connections may come from such a free-wheeling process but it is not the disciplined application of left-brain thinking to a specific issue that is blocking your progress. When you use technical reading as specific resource we suggest you write down your intention as part of that week's mental training programme in your log book.

Trigger books

One of the British cycling team takes time before each race to read a couple of pages of Tolkien's *Lord of the Rings*. He says this is not simply to calm him down to the right level of excitement but more exactly it helps him to contact a particular feeling or mood that he always has when he produces his best performance. It's hard for him to describe this feeling but that's of no importance. He knows what he needs and he knows how to gain access to it.

Barbara Potter, the long time world top-ten computed tennis player, does a similar exercise. Her book is called *The Ways of a Sword*. She has carried it around on the circuit for years and it is severely underlined, page after page. When questioned about it, she replied simply 'This is my Bible.'

Many people the world over prepare themselves for a night's sleep by reading a passage from the Bible itself. Many others have a favourite bedside book that helps them to access a relaxed frame of mind or comforts them if they wake or makes them smile when they're feeling depressed. To exploit this exercise fully, you would compose a library of books, each of which evoked the particular mood you require for a particular performance or for a particular moment in the course of that performance.

Thinking of your performance: associative exercises

Visualisation

Visualisation, sometimes called the use of mental imagery or imaging, is the deliberate and cultivated use of our ability to evoke mentally a performance or a scene, as if it is being experienced here and now. Effective visualisation includes not just what you can see but also what you can hear, touch, smell, taste and, most importantly, what it feels like kinaesthetically to 'be there'.

Visualisation is probably the most dramatic way of thinking to win. We are all taught to use our analytical left brain, to think *about* our performance, at an early age. The use of 'right-brain' techniques – thinking *of* our performance – has developed rapidly over the past decade and become widespread in the world of sport. It is a technique, developed from psychosynthesis, that we have fostered over the years.

Everyone has the capacity to visualise – but it is a capacity that can be developed. Some people take to it more easily than others but the process can be used effectively by everyone. In fact, to some extent, it's true to say that we all visualise whether we know it or not. A few athletes such as the England football player Glenn Hoddle who had never heard of the skill until we described it, have instinctively developed a preparation ritual that includes a form of visualisation. Many others, and this is true of sports people and non-sports performers alike, have a habit of rehearsing their mistakes – playing them over again and again, fixing them well in their mind. Just by including visualisation in your mental training programme or personal business plan, you will become more aware of any tendency towards negative visualisation and your performance will improve.

Visualisation uses the language of the body – the body's sensations of feeling, seeing, hearing, smell, temperature, colour, movement, touch and taste. It bypasses the analytical mind and directly affects both your emotional and physical functioning. When you visualise yourself moving, the muscle groups involved in such an action actually move on a subliminal level as your visualisation sends small messages through your nervous system to those muscles.

To visualise effectively, follow these guidelines:

- sit down and let yourself relax, at least when the situation allows and when learning the exercise. Visualising when you're tense means your muscles get contradictory messages.

- stay alert. This means don't lie down unless you are feeling wide awake and full of energy. You'll be able to visualise but may not be able to control and direct your visualisation.

- have a specific goal. Decide in advance what skill you want to improve and choose a specific short example of having performed that skill well.

- have a realistic goal. Don't imagine yourself playing a hole in one. Focus on some element of your swing and see the ball leave the club on course and land as it does when you play your best.

- use all your senses. Remember that visualisation is not just *seeing* with the mind's eye but also hearing, touching, tasting, smelling and recalling how it feels kinaesthetically to perform in this way.

- visualise from inside, rather than watching yourself as if from outside. This helps you to evoke the kinaesthetic sense.

- visualise at the correct speed, except when you want to focus on a specific element of the movement. (Of course you may not be visualising movement at all.)

- practise regularly. Five minutes a day, once a day for ten days or two weeks is a good start.

- enjoy it. This is all important. If you allow any mental training exercise to become a chore, it will not serve you well. If you allow visualisation practice to become a pain, because you are relaxed, some element of that pain may enter into your actual performance later on.

Now for the various types of visualisation. There are two main categories and several examples of each. We call the two categories, (a) mental rehearsal, which involves rehearsing and improving a movement and (b) problem-solving, which is used to improve a number of other performance skills, particularly those we called mental skills in the Skills Assessment exercise (p. 43).

Mental rehearsal

Performance practice   This is the basic mental rehearsal exercise of a particular performance skill. You recall a time in the past when you did perform this skill well or you recall seeing someone else perform this skill well (and eventually imagine you *are* that person performing the skill) or you recall yourself doing something similar well or the same thing in a different situation and make a transposition. It is an exercise you would normally do at home although not necessarily if circumstances dictate otherwise.

A variation on the straight performance practice rehearsal is used when you can't recall *ever* performing the way you wish to perform. In this case, visualise someone else performing the skill perfectly – someone you have seen perform in real life, on film or on television. Begin by imagining that you are watching this person and then imagine that you *are* the person, are inside their body performing as they can perform and experiencing how it feels to perform like that. This type of performance practice is called 'Ideal Model'.

Instant preplay   This varies from performance practice in that it is done immediately before your performance, in the place of your performance. Greg Lougarnis the twice double Olympic Champion diver (1984 and 1988) rehearsed each dive whilst he stood poised above the water. On a more mundane level, if you have a difficult phone call to make, rehearse your opening words and tone as you sit with your hand ready on the instrument. If you have a difficult personal message to communicate, rehearse how you will express yourself, without allowing any interruption.

As If visualisation   This visualisation is practised *whilst* you perform, with a view to improving a specific quality of performance. If you are a waiter and feel your performance is too clumsy, name the quality you feel is the opposite to clumsiness and then get an image for that quality. If the quality you choose is 'grace', then think of something or someone that/who expresses that perfectly. Then, as you perform your job that evening, imagine for a few minutes at a time that you *are* that thing or person that expresses the quality so well.

Modelling   An off-shoot of the Ideal Model and the As If visualisation, modelling builds a new pattern based on the behaviour of some one else. You act out some of the attributes of another individual, thereby enhancing your own behaviour.

First you decide upon a skill which needs improving or a quality which can be enhanced. Then you choose an individual who performs that skill ideally or embodies the chosen quality. Then relax, close your eyes and imagine how it would *feel* like to be the person you've chosen and act the way that he or she acts. Later on you actually act as if you are that person, experiencing the new way of being and noticing the feelings it evokes. When you 'are' this person, what words do you use? How do you speak? How do you stand? How do you move?

Modelling is one of the most effective modes of recreating beliefs and attitudes. It's also an enjoyable way to change your behaviour. Sometimes, when you take your model from a different sphere of activity, you find the exercise to be particularly enlightening. We've had tennis players modelling themselves on Margaret Thatcher and businessmen on Glenn Hoddle or Joe Montana.

Modelling can be practised in one-off situations or it can form the basis for a sustained change of behaviour. It can also be used as a stepping stone, by modelling a series of individuals and capturing a quality or skill from each. In this case you build your own composite model as the basis for your new pattern of behaviour.

Instant replay   The reverse of instant preplay, instant replay, involves rehearsing a particular skill immediately after you have performed it well, to fix in your 'bodymind' the memory of how it felt to do it right.

For example, you were fascinated by the juggler you saw on the beach last summer, have bought three dog balls and have tried for days without success to get the third ball into the air without dropping the other two. Suddenly you do it: each ball travels from your hand in turn, up into the air, safely down to the other hand and up again as the next ball arrives . . . one, two, three, four, five times before you drop one! Stop at that point, close your eyes, take a deep breath; let it out slowly and standing as you are, with your eyes closed, rehearse the whole sequence you just made and exactly how it felt. Then open your eyes and start again.

Performance review   The reverse of performance practice, this type of mental rehearsal is done at home at the end of the day and consists of a complete visual review of the salient points of the performance. Dwell on the positive points but note the negative moments and rehearse instead how you *should* have performed them.

Problem-solving visualisations

Black Box visualisation   We developed this visualisation exercise when working with Barbara Lynch in 1979, who later became the European clay-pigeon shooting champion. It is an exercise to aid concentration when you are either surrounded by distractions you can't do anything about or you are full of distracting feelings.

First identify the distractions, close your eyes and relax, take a deep breath in, hold it a moment and let it go very slowly, allowing each muscle group of your body in turn to rest – from your face down to your feet – you imagine you are in a room on your own sitting at a desk or table, looking out of the window.

Then you look down at the desk, see a sheet of paper and a pen and you write a list of all the distractions you previously identified. You then fold the piece of paper, turn and see a box with a lid close by. You open the box, put the piece of paper inside, close it and turn back to the desk, sitting back in your chair and looking out of the window.

Quiet Place visualisation   This exercise is one to help you deal with stress and anxiety. Sit back in your chair, close your eyes, relax and imagine you are out of doors in some peaceful place on your own, maybe in a field by a river, by the sea, in the mountains or in a forest. Notice what position you're in, then if necessary move slightly so that whilst still being comfortable you can see the line of the horizon or whatever is in front of you. Look at the ground, touch the ground, rub your fingers on the ground and lift them to your nose. Let your hand fall, turn to the left and see what objects, shapes and colours there are there, noticing the play of light and shadow, the time of day, the season of the year and being aware of the weather and how that feels.

Then turn to the right, see what is there, what shapes and colours and notice what sounds there are that belong to the place. Look above, look behind you and then settle back into your original position, looking at the horizon and noticing how it feels to be there, where you can't be disturbed (unless you so choose) and where there is nothing in particular that you have to do . . .

Once you get to your Quiet Place quite easily, you can begin to use it to solve certain problems. In this case, you close your eyes, relax and get an image of your problem, so that it is represented by some thing or living creature, perhaps a person, a stranger or friend. Then go to your Quiet Place and invite this image to come there to you. Once it is close by, begin to talk to this image: 'Who are you? What do you want? What do you need? What different ways might you get your needs met?' When you have some answers, let the image leave your Quiet Place. Rest there a while reflecting on the conversation and then open your eyes and write down in your log book what happened and what answers you got.

The Wise Old Person   This is another visualisation that is used to find the answers to certain problems. Sit down, close your eyes and relax. Imagine you are in a field on your own in the warm sunshine. Turn around and in the near distance you'll see a mountain. Walk across the field in that direction till you reach a gate and turn left along the path beyond the hedge outside. After a short time you'll get to a cross-path with a sign pointing to the right which says 'THE WAY TO FIND OUT'. Follow this path and soon the ground rises. Then the hedges fall away and the path begins to climb, steeper and steeper till you're zigzagging up the side of the mountain.

As you reach the top you see a structure. You go inside and there you meet a Wise Old Person. You explain your problem and ask a question. The Wise Old Person gives you a reply and hands you something which you take back with you down the mountain. When you get back to the field you look carefully at what the Wise Old Person gave you.

Then come back to the room, open your eyes and write down what the Wise Old Person said. Then write down a description of the thing you received, without naming it. Write down any new thoughts you have about your problem. Write down any connection you can find between your gift and your problem. And, finally, reread your description of your gift and see how far the description corresponds to a description of yourself. What further insight to your problem do you get from this?

The Subpersonality Bus   This exercise helps you to distinguish between your wants and your needs and to discover ways in which you can constructively meet your needs thereby reducing any obstacle and improving your performance.

Sit back, close your eyes, take a deep breath and let it out slowly. As you do so, allow each muscle group in your body, from head down to feet, relax. Then imagine that you are out of doors in a field. Feel the warmth of the sun and watch the breeze play across the grass. Begin to cross the field and soon you'll see that it is bordered on the side you're approaching by an old bumpy road. As you watch, a rickety bus drives up. On the front of the bus, instead of its destination, it says 'SUBPERSONALITIES'. The bus stops, the door opens and out step several people – notice what they are like, how they are dressed, how they move, what you imagine they are and how you feel you should refer to them.

One of them walks across the field towards you and you sit down together. You ask it who it is and it gives you a name that describes its character. You become aware of what this person needs, what it wants and what it has to offer. You reply to what you've just learned and together you take decisions for the future.

When you've finished your conversation, come back to the room, open your eyes and spend a while writing down what happened, what was said and what decisions you took.

The people who came out of the bus are subpersonalities and manifestations of certain positive qualities such as love, judgement, power, service, humour, creativity, discrimination and so on. However, to begin with, when you first encounter your subpersonalities you find that they can't represent the quality they embody very well. Instead they are, to a greater or lesser degree, subpersonality distortions.

One way of giving more substance to new patterns and beliefs is to discover and explore the subpersonalities which embody them. We suggest that you work with a subpersonality (i) when it has needs and wants which must be met before you can fully utilise its potential (ii) when you want to stand back from it and move on to a more appropriate pattern of behaviour (iii) when you want to discover the hidden meanings and untapped potential in a pattern and utilise it more consciously or (iv) when you want to cultivate a subpersonality in order to introduce a pattern which is new or not fully operational.

Visual re-editing   This exercise is to help you overcome a past unpleasant memory. Sit down, close your eyes and relax. Play the memory through once, just as it happened. Then reflect a moment. What else should or might have happened that would have been positive? At what point in the sequence of events would the difference have begun to occur? Go back to the beginning of the original memory, set the scene again as it was, then allow the event to unfold but at the right moment let things change and happen positively, just as you imagined just now. Play this new positive version two or three times and again each day for five minutes for a couple of weeks. The idea is not to deny the past but to create new positive responses for the future, when you might find yourself in a similar situation again.

Pictures

It would be possible to build a gallery of pictures, taken from magazines, one that represented for you a perfect example of each of the physical, technical and mental skills of your performance. Usually though the exercise is just to find a picture that represents a perfect example of the skill that you need to improve right now. So, if the skill scoring highest on your Skills Assessment exercise was concentration, you'd find a picture which either helped you to concentrate or is of some one that you felt was concentrating perfectly. You'd then put it on your wall for a couple of weeks only, whilst you did other physical and technical and mental training exercises to improve that particular skill.

Drawing or painting a picture yourself is a similar exercise with the added advantage that you focus even more intently on the thing or person presented. This is particularly good for problem solving or clarifying and holding your Vision.

Collages

Making a collage has the same advantages as drawing or painting a picture. Another way of exploiting this medium is to do an exercise called **Inside–Outside** in which you stick pictures which represent you as you imagine you are seen by others on the outside of a foolscap size envelope. You then cut out another set of pictures that represent how you think you really are and put them inside the envelope. You then sit down with a friend or co-worker who has done the same thing, explain your envelopes to each other and give feedback to each other as to how you felt when you heard your partner's self-description.

Video

Having a video made of your performance and watching it afterwards can be a useful mental training exercise, whether you watch it alone or with a coach, a superior or a colleague or team mate. However, you should watch a video selectively and infrequently. The advantage of a video is that it gives an exact record of what you did and can remind you both of aspects of your performance that were good and need to be repeated more often and of aspects that were bad and need to be eliminated.

The disadvantages of a video are twofold. Firstly, it does not convey the kinaesthetic sense of your performance and if you view it too often you will find it difficult to access that element of your memory any more – the outside view will overlay your actual memory too heavily. This happened to Mark Falco when we were working at Tottenham Hotspur Football Club. He scored one goal in a Cup competition that was so remarkable that the television showed it what seemed like dozens of times within a few days. This would have been an important memory for him to use at a later date but he said that he had seen the television replay too often and could no longer remember what it *felt* like.

Secondly, viewed more than once, the video will begin to reinforce any mistake that is shown on the film. To avoid this, on the first viewing, you should note down any mistakes that you want to correct and then work on them one at a time. In each case, this will involve doing a visual re-editing visualisation: playing the memory back to the point where things began to go wrong and then substituting an image of you doing what you should have done or would have liked to have done (as long as this is realistic). Having got a new version of the incident, you should practise it for five minutes each day for ten days.

Physical images

A physical image is any object which inspires the feeling you want to have when you perform. It is something which for you is the image of success, the image of confidence, the image of patience or whatever. It could be a trophy, it could be a framed certificate, it could be a small buddha you brought back from India one year. It may of course be something that you have permanently on display and represents a particular quality in your life.

To use these objects effectively you should either find something that evokes the feeling or quality especially for the occasion or else you move something you already have on display to a new position, so that you become more aware of it. In either case you place the image there for just ten days to two weeks – the length of time that you spend working on improving that particular quality in your performance.

Mental images

This exercise involves developing an image or symbol for a quality you want to express in your performance. If you want to be more assertive, perhaps you'll choose a tiger; if you want to be more agile, you might think of a gazelle; if you want to be

more patient perhaps it'll be a mountain. You can spend time
energising this symbol by visualising it, drawing it or cutting
out pictures of it from Sunday newspaper colour supplements.
Then, on the pitch, in the meeting or during your presentation,
you can act as if you are this symbol or imagine it by your side.
In this way, you begin to identify with the new and substitute
your action, symbol, language or mental imagery for the old
undesired pattern.

Substitution

Your mind is the repository of a wealth of past experience. It
creates context and meaning as well as supplying most of the
content of your daily reality. It is never empty. As anyone
who has tried concentration or meditation techniques knows,
it is very difficult to create a blank space in your mind. As
fast as one's memory, thought, feeling, sensation or fantasy
fades, others come rushing in. When you have managed to
rid yourself of an old thought-form, prejudice or bad memory
make sure that you substitute something positive, otherwise the
old negative patterns and problems will reassert themselves.

If you are driving down a rutted driveway, the wheels of your
car are naturally going to follow the ruts. You can steer your car
on to the verge but, unless you fill the ruts in, the likelihood
is that your car will soon slip back into the old path. Prayer is
probably the oldest form of mental substitution practised. If
the devout follower doesn't want thoughts of the material and
sensory pleasures of the world to intrude, he or she fills the
space with religious words and ritual. Once you have become
aware of a pattern you want to change, create the correct new
pattern and repeat it as often as possible.

Metaphor

This exercise involves using images, story telling, analogy and
anecdotes. It presents a picture of what is going on in a new

way. When you use a metaphor you connect with something very different from your present view of the situation. It disassociates you from the trap in which you find yourself. At the moment you are thinking in a certain way and using a certain language to describe your current position. Yet it is that language, that way of thinking about the information that you have, together with the problem-solving techniques you are using, which ensures that you stay stuck in the problem. Metaphor kicks your thinking sideways. It propels your mind through the looking-glass. In order to find your way back you have to discover a connection between objects and ideas not normally associated in your thoughts.

If you tell yourself: 'I have a trade union problem', you'll automatically think of the normal solutions – mediation, arbitration and negotiation. But if instead you get an image or metaphor for the situation and say: 'I've got a problem like a porcupine or a hedgehog – how should I deal with it', you begin to think of handling it 'with gloves' or 'with a shovel' or 'with a bag or sack'. Each of these new responses could be translated back into a tactic like 'going gently', or 'keeping them at arm's length' or 'surrounding them'.

Similarly if you have a problem with your concentration you might think of the metaphor: 'My concentration is like a rabbit bouncing all over the place'. Then your response might be to 'feed it', 'cage it', or 'find it another rabbit', which might translate back into the tactics: 'give it something *pleasurable* to focus on', 'get boundaries – large or small – to control it' or 'practise concentration exercises with a friend.'

Storytelling

Storytelling is another way to arrive at a different level of meaning. Many of the best storytellers are to be found in the Bible. Jesus almost always used allegory and parables to convey clear messages. The language in which their thoughts were expressed heavily predisposed them to conform to their

religion and their law. Many of the early stories in the Old
Testament are allegories – for example the story of creation
or the Book of Job. Stories such as these cause us to reflect on
our lives and experiences in a new way leading to a new level
of understanding. *Aesop's Fables* still convey meaning through
metaphor and allegory.

Sport and business are also full of metaphors. In fact it's
interesting to notice how far sport and business are metaphors
for each other! How many times have you heard the expression
'welcome aboard' in a context other than sailing? For a
newcomer to a commercial organisation, such a metaphor
gives a strong secondary message, one like 'we're all in
this together' or 'we have a tight set of rules here which
we expect you to pick up soon.' Conversely, in professional
football, 'Okay, you're the boss' or 'The boss says so, that's
why' carries the clear implication that the manager or coach
is an authoritarian leader. Metaphors provoke a new level of
awareness in relation to an old situation.

Mascots

A mascot is an object which inspires the feeling you want to have
when you perform. However it is used on a semi-permanent
basis and is usually considered (if only half seriously) to attract
good luck and ward off bad. It is usually personified and given
a name. The great diver, Greg Lougarnis, had a teddy bear
he called 'Gar the Bear' with whom he played and to whom
he talked (by his own admission) between dives in any major
competition.

There is a story of another American Olympic champion,
a long-jumper who appeared before the world press after the
medal ceremony, with his teddy bear which he put carefully on
the chair beside him. After answering all the questions, he was
getting up to leave when one journalist asked 'Excuse me, but
what is that teddy bear doing beside you?' The athlete smiled
and replied, 'I wondered if any of you were going to ask that.

That's my bear, *he* actually won the medal, not I.' 'What do you mean?' asked the journalist. 'Well', replied the athlete 'you remember there was one more jump after the one that won me the medal, a jump to be made by the Russian who was in second place? Well, as the Russian came in for that final jump, I turned my bear to face him and said 'Get him . . . and, of course, he did a foul jump, didn't he?'

If you decide to get a mascot to inspire you to good performances, don't just choose the first thing that comes to hand. It must be something with a strong positive association. Something appropriate that is given to you by someone you trust, respect and love would be ideal. In a way, a mascot is similar to Greek worry beads. In a crisis or even at other times during the day, the Greek will fish out his leather thong of beads and, either intentionally or absent mindedly, will begin to count.

Rituals

Worry beads, of course, have a religious connotation and religion is full of rituals which inspire the faithful to spiritual perceptions. There may indeed be an important spiritual element to your performance. However, there are other rituals whose effectiveness, like the use of mascots is more related to superstition.

Graham Roberts, a former Tottenham Hotspur football player, had to be last out of the dressing room, when the team left to go down through the tunnel and out on to the pitch. If any other player was lingering in the lavatory or taking time to give a last tug to his laces, Graham would tell him to get on with it. Graham felt that by leaving the dressing room last he was doing all he could to ensure he had a good game.

There is no harm in the superstitious element of rituals and mascots except that there may obviously be a day when your mascot is packed in the bag that the airline has lost or, as in Graham's case, when you move to another club and find

someone already there has the same ritual. The answer then
of course is to identify the feeling that such a ritual or mascot
has been giving you and then use some other mental training
exercise to evoke that same feeling.

There is an important non-superstitious aspect of ritual. This
involves evolving a strictly ordered attentional pattern which
you adopt just prior to your performance. It is the type of
personal ritual that all great tennis players so obviously display
just before they serve (bouncing the ball a set number of times,
looking at their opponent, bouncing the ball again, and so on)
and also just before they receive service (shifting from foot to
foot). If you have to give speeches and want to improve your
performance, you should evolve a ritual for the moments before
you begin to speak.

Music

The use of music is another evocative mental training exercise.
It is one that appeals strongly to most athletes we've worked
with and one which they find easy to use. It is also one which
may be easily applied to your own performance, in whatever
field that may be. Whichever skill you wish to improve, go
back to a time when you performed that skill well – the best
that you remember having performed it. Do a **Performance
review** visualisation of that occasion and then ask yourself
'What is the quality of this performance that I'm rehearsing?'
and come up with a word like 'smooth', 'easy', 'powerful' or
some other word of the same class. Then ask yourself 'What for
me is smooth music?' or 'What for me is easy music' or 'What
for me is smooth music?' and allow some particular song or
tune or other piece of music to come to mind.

Then for the next ten days or two weeks, as you work
at programmes of other training exercises to improve the
particular skill, make sure that you (i) find time to actually
listen to this piece of music and (ii) decide when, before or
during your performance, it would be particularly helpful to

evoke that quality. Having taken the decision, play the music through your head at those times – again for the next couple of weeks only.

Mike Brearley it is said, when captaining the England cricket team successfully, helped himself give a courageous and steadfast performance at the wicket against the speed of the West Indian bowlers by humming hymn tunes to himself. One of the Glamorgan batsmen we worked with in 1987 wanted to improve his patience at the wicket. He prepared for the occasion at home by listening to 'We are the World' on his stereo and then played through his mind 'You don't Bring Me Flowers' by Barbra Streisand as he strode out to the wicket – having previously identified those tunes as giving him a feeling of patience.

The cyclist Ben Luckwell, one of the 1988 British Olympic team time trialists, wanted to improve his ability to remain 'relaxed and clear' on the line before the start and find additional strength and power over the last kilometre. He chose to play through his mind 'I'm Still Waiting' by Diana Ross, as he waited on the line, and 'Beat Surrender' by the Jam during his final effort.

Relaxation exercises

The ability to relax is an essential skill for any performer, in business or sport, in teaching or dance, for a judge or a dustman. Until you are able to relax, you cannot really withdraw, become the observer, and think intelligently either of or about your performance. Relaxation exercises are therefore included in this list.

Our own technique has been derived from hatha yoga and consists of allowing one muscle group to rest after another – from the head down to the feet if sitting and from the feet up to the head, if lying down – whilst allying the process to an awareness of one's breath. Begin by closing your eyes, putting your feet flat on the floor and your hands easily in your lap (if you are sitting down). Listen for a moment to the sounds you can hear outside of the room, then bring your attention into the stillness of the room itself and then further inside to awareness of your physical position and the contact you make with the chair. Take a deeper breath, hold it for the count of four, then let it go very slowly, maybe to the count of eight. Then as you continue breathing normally, pay attention to the muscles of your face – your forehead, your eyes, the muscles around your eyes, your cheeks, your mouth, your jaw, your neck and imagine any tension draining away through your shoulders, through your arms, wrists, hands, thumbs and fingers.

Notice that your chest is relaxed, your back, your stomach, waist and pelvis. Pay attention to your thighs, stay with any tension you may find and then, on the next outbreath, imagine it draining away through your knees, through your calves, through your ankles, through your feet and into the floor – leaving you calm, relaxed and alert. And you remain in this state for a few minutes before stretching and opening your eyes again. If you have included a mental rehearsal in your mental training programme, doing it immediately after your relaxation is particularly effective.

Other reliable methods of relaxation are Shultz's Autogenic Training and Jacobsen's Progressive Relaxation.

Acting

The ability to act, to step confidently into a role, to experience that role and play it convincingly is something you should use and develop. For a start there is always at least one per cent of the actor who is an observer. He retains the ability to step out of his performance when necessary and this in turn allows him to see ways in which his performance can be improved.

If there is a particular quality you want to develop, try acting like someone who you feel embodies that quality, or as an animal or bird who epitomises that quality for you.

There is also a Gestalt acting game called the **Chair Dialogue** which allows you to get a certain insight into your relationship with a superior, co-worker, subordinate, pupil or team mate, with whom you have difficulty. This exercise involves you sitting in a chair opposite a second chair that is empty, and speaking to that chair as if the person concerned is sitting in it. Tell that person all your wants and needs, your gripes, your moans and your resentments. Make demands as if he or she were really there.

When you have finished, change chairs. Pretend you are that person and give your response to everything that has just been said. Make what you imagine this person's response would be, what he or she wants and needs, what gripes resentments and demands he or she has. Make them as if you were that person talking to yourself. When you've said everything change back to your original chair and continue the dialogue, changing chairs as your mind dictates until you find each of the two characters, 'yourself' and 'the other person' beginning to express appreciation of each other for certain strengths. By the time you've got this far, you'll have found a new way to view and work with your relationship.

Two exercises already described – the **As If** visualisation and working with a **subpersonality** – can be extended by acting. If you identify a subpersonality that you want to strengthen, bring its nature increasingly into focus by discovering key phrases, images and actions associated with it. Then go into real life situations, acting as if you *are* that subpersonality, with all its attributes and characteristics. You do this exercise for five minutes, or on and off all day if you find it helps.

It's not always easy to introduce and maintain new patterns of behaviour and new attitudes about yourself and the world at large. To do this successfully you need to change your self-image, your emotions and feelings, your thought patterns and even your body movements – only then will your new patterns stick. Finding a subpersonality that can act as a vehicle for this new way of being can be a most efficient way of doing this.

It's important to remember that the role or subpersonality embodies the fundamental quality you want to strengthen in yourself. Make sure that quality is one that reflects your Vision and is in some way part of your unexpressed potential.

Energising the opposite

This is another acting exercise. Having become aware of some aspects of your behaviour which is too exaggerated to be effective and is therefore counter-productive, stop for a moment and ask yourself what the *opposite* behaviour would be. Then identify who for you demonstrates this behaviour and act it out. The more you exaggerate, the more likely you are to become aware of the happy medium between the two polarities and to tone down your own original behaviour to a more acceptable and effective level.

People

As you develop your performance methodically from week to week and month to month, through mental training, you'll find yourself building not just a library of books, musical tapes and a gallery of pictures that you can draw upon as and when you need to evoke a particular skill or quality of performance. You will also be building a gallery of friends and acquaintances who seem to embody these same skills and qualities.

At first it is easier to see the qualities you need to develop in yourself 'out there' in other people. 'He is confident and gives me a feeling of confidence', you'll think. Okay, so when you need to increase your confidence prior to some important performance, go and spend some time with this person. If you are a team performer and the person is a team mate, so much the better. As you perform, you might think of this person or even for moments, act as if you are him. Eventually though, you'll begin to own these projected qualities and experience and express them directly as yours.

Associative problem–solving

Some problems, usually non-people ones, are particularly amenable to linear problem solving. Use verbal analytical processes with those problems. However, in a world of ever-increasing change, innovation and uncertainty, success depends on meeting like with like wherever possible. We suggest that you begin to explore some of the new more radical right-brain approaches to problem-solving as soon as you can.

You may have already found that your problem-solving process has required you to leave your usual linear approach. Do you have to draw or cut out pictures? Does it break away from columns and lines? Does it ask you to identify aspects of your problem and work with them through assuming different roles or taking excursions into imagery? Does it break down old concepts and ideas? If so, jump aboard and begin to see how changing over to thinking *of* the problem rather than thinking *about* it can move you beyond your old understandings and interpretations.

One way to think *of* your problem is to turn the whole situation into an **allegory** or fairy story, creating characters to represent each of the different factors that contribute to the problem, naming yourself as the leading protagonist. By elaborating on the characters or events you can highlight them and discover some other level of meaning to their actions. As a result, many of the hidden or unconscious factors which are perpetuating the current conflict begin to emerge.

An associative problem-solving exercise that combines with other **people** is **brainstorming**. Here you present your problem to two or more friends and then all suggest solutions. For brainstorming to work several rules have to be followed meticulously.

- One person writes or scribes for the team

- The team members offer as many ideas as come into their minds

- Everyone contributes

- There are no wrong ideas – all ideas count and are written down except where they repeat other ideas

- You can build on ideas already offered

- Keep the pace brisk

- There is a set time limit – usually two to five minutes after which the brainstorming session stops

After the session you can then evaluate the ideas (no evaluation during the session) and select the ones you want to pursue. This is done through discussion, polling or voting, the 'client' who has responsibility for action selecting the ideas or seeking consensus. Remember, brainstorming usually needs to be followed by decision making and developing steps to implement the ideas.

11
Strategies for change

Are you now 'thinking to win'? Have you managed to incorporate some effective mental training exercises into your daily routine? If so, it is important that you review your experience and reflect on what you have done. This chapter outlines some of the theory behind the change process.

There are five stages in the process of change or six if you include getting your Vision and goalsetting. The five final stages are **awareness**, **disidentification**, **reframing**, **recreating** and **synthesising**. Each of these stages has several different processes which lead towards your objective and towards implementing change. Although none of these stages are obligatory, and although you didn't necessarily have to go through then in sequence, they are each a step in the process of creating change. Our experience is that lasting change occurs when you can be seen to have followed this process.

If you have used this book to evaluate your lifetime goals you will have followed this sequence quite closely, but if you were dealing with a problem as specific as improving your tennis backhand or your presentation skills, you may not have followed all the steps, particularly if you had already taken several of them before reaching for this book. Similarly you won't have needed to use *all* the mental training exercises listed in the last chapter. However, the more fundamental the change you were seeking to create, the more helpful it should be to review your experience in the light of this process.

Awareness or (what's so)

In our consultancy, Sporting Bodymind Ltd, we have a common expression, adopted from Gestalt psychology. The phrase is 'what's so', and can be used as a statement or a question.

Examples of such statements would be:

'What's so is that your foremen don't agree with the changes you want.'

'What's so is, no matter how much you practise, your putting continues to deteriorate.'

'What's so is whether or not you think you're listening, you haven't heard what she said',

'What's so is you want to move to a new house',

'What's so is What's so'. (Tautological but descriptive and about the situation as it is now.)

We also use 'What's so' as a question. Two co-workers are arguing about whose responsibility it was to submit a proposal on time after a deadline has passed. The argument could go on endlessly. 'What's so?' we ask, and one co-worker replies: 'What's so is I thought he was responsible and I feel let down.' 'Oh!' we say 'So what's so *now* is that you feel let down.'

Or a golfer confides: 'What's so is that I want to win the medal competition next month.' 'Okay', we say, 'what's so for you now?' 'What's so' replies the golfer 'is that I need to improve my driving in order to have a shot at the medal.'

At the beginning of this book you went through a systematic evaluation of your objective. This visioning and goalsetting stage was crucial to devising a mental training programme: your strategies and tactics had to be designed to meet future needs as well as solving current problems. If you've got a Vision, if you've set goals for an extended period of time and evaluated those goals to establish priorities and direction, you will have established What's so for you. For the organisational problem solver this is called getting a problem statement and a problem description: it ensures that you're solving the right problem! It requires that you clarify your point of departure and where you want to go before you embark on a mental training programme. It's like doing a marketing survey on yourself. You're the customer: you find out what *you* want (now and in the future).

After defining your Vision and setting your goals, you asked the question 'What's so?' on a more pragmatic level: what were your current strengths and weaknesses? Which of the physical, technical and mental skills that are part of your performance did you need most to improve? What obstacles did you put or were put in your path? And what inner and outer resources do you have at your disposal?

We have worked with many intuitive people in both sport and business who were able to see straight to the heart of a problem and find an instant solution. Intuition is good when it works but questioning as a process often gets further beneath the surface to real issues. On it's own it may not be enough for you to implement, never mind maintain, a systematic programme for change, but having found out what's so, you'll have prepared the ground for a programme that will address the basic issues.

As an American, I (Christopher Connolly) discovered the true importance of asking 'what's so' almost inadvertently, when we were invited to work with our first First Division football club. At that time, I knew little about the technical and tactical aspects of the British game, so when we met the players and coaches I was continually asking questions. 'What is a midfielder's role? What is a set piece? What does a sweeper do in the team? Why do you have the team sit in a row? When do midfield and defence communicate?' 'What do they say to each other?' and so forth. Questions like these increased my awareness but more significantly they increased the awareness of the team. Players began to reexamine their roles and relationships with positive results. Ten years later, we hear this form of questioning is described in the management consultancy world as 'naive listening'.

Awareness is fundamental to change. We live in a fast moving world where action is frequently valued ahead of all else. Yet one of our clients, the training manager of a large multinational corporation has confided to us 'If there was one thing I'd like to have more than anything else, it's time for reflection. More than a bigger budget, a bigger head count, even than recognition from the Vice President, I need time to take stock of where we are at, time to look at what we've accomplished and to evaluate our current initiatives. Then I could really begin to anticipate the future, to plan for the changes in our workforce, for the new systems we are implementing and the management initiatives just around the corner.'

Disidentification

Disidentification, the second stage in creating change, was the point at which you were asked to stop believing, expressing yourself and acting according to your old patterns. You had to do this in order to create room for the new. It is the stage at which you became aware that you are in control and have the ability to rehearse your course of action.

We all act in accordance with beliefs and attitudes which we have learned and cultivated over many years. Like physical skills, they are learned emotional and mental responses, based upon past experience. They become essential: without attitudes and beliefs we would have to relearn our response to each situation each time it occurred. These attitudes have become ingrained in our minds and, indeed in our nervous systems.

The problem will have arisen when you wanted to change those responses. If they are physical habits like stepping forward when you should step back in cricket, forgetting to follow through in tennis, or always taking the ball on the left foot in football, the disidentification process will have involved a mental stop, some kind of relaxation technique and a refocusing on a task-orientated skill. For closed skills like a high-board dive, a gymnastics vault, a penalty kick, a basketball free throw, it may have involved rehearsing the fault once mentally, a brief breathing exercise and then rehearsing the skill as it should happen.

For attitudes and beliefs the process is similar but more complicated. The first step in disidentification is already taken in the awareness or 'what's so?' stage of the change process. It is here that you first begin to distance yourself from old concepts and beliefs. You perhaps have gained a new level of understanding of your situation so see it in a new light. Maybe you have discovered resources you didn't know you had and suddenly you no longer see yourself as being stuck in the situation with no choices.

You may have gone through an exercise that develops the observer in you and so realise that what you have been experiencing is not the whole story. As a result you have begun to gain distance from the old image you had of yourself, from your old story and the confines of your old choices: you have begun to disidentify.

Another way towards disidentification is to make clear statements that *you* are not those old patterns that you want to change. Statements like 'I'm not a slow starter', 'I'm not my habitual reactions', 'I'm not my unconscious problems' are simple verbal disidentifications which allow you to realise that you are more than the old and you have room to identify with the new. This process helps you to identify with your observer, what we call the 'I'. As you build the connection with your 'I' you begin to realise that while the 'I' or observer doesn't have any content, it can be used to change the context by focusing your attention on to the thoughts, ideas, experiences, actions and patterns which you want to develop and cultivate. By disidentifying from the old, you prepare the ground for expressing the new.

The third step of disidentification is turning your full

attention to the new. You focus your inner eye in the direction you want to go. You may not yet fully embody the new way of doing things but you have begun to direct your energy towards the positive. Instead of looking at where you have been, you can now look at where you are going.

As you followed the book, you may have done this by redefining your Vision statement or by using some of the mental training exercises described in the last chapter, such as mentally rehearsing the action you were about to perform or finding a positive sentence that expressed your intent. As you chose your way you will have found yourself focusing on the direction of the new.

Disidentification always involves a choice, an act of will. It is a conscious process, not something you can do habitually. You choose to stop focusing your attention on the old. You deliberately draw in your attention and connect with your 'I' or observer. From here you can view old patterns in a new way, integrating those new actions that you want to implement.

Reframing

Reframing is changing the meaning given to an experience without changing the experience itself. Paul Watzlawick gives us an example from Mark Twain's *Huckleberry Finn*.

> It is Saturday afternoon, holiday time for all boys, except Tom Sawyer, who has been sentenced to whitewash thirty yards of board fence nine feet high. Life to him seems hollow, and existence but a burden. It is not only the work that he finds intolerable, but especially the thought of all the boys who will be coming along and making fun of him for having work. At this dark and hopeless moment an inspiration burst upon him! Nothing less than a great, magnificent inspiration. Soon enough a boy comes in sight, the very boy, of all boys, whose ridicule he had been dreading most: 'Hello, old

> chap, you got to work, hey?' 'Why, it's you, Ben!
> I warn't noticing.' 'Say, – I'm going a-swimming, I
> am. Don't you wish you could? But of course you'd
> ruther work – wouldn't you? Course you would!' Tom
> contemplated the boy a bit, and said: 'What do you
> call work?' 'Why, ain't that work?' Tom resumed his
> whitewashing, and answered carelessly: 'Well, maybe
> it is, and maybe it ain't. All I know, is, it suits Tom
> Sawyer.' 'Oh come, now you don't mean to let on that
> you like it?' The brush continued to move. 'Like it?
> Well, don't see why I oughtn't to like it. Does a boy
> get a chance to whitewash a fence every day?' That
> put the thing in a new light. Ben stopped nibbling his
> apple. Tom swept his brush daintily back and forth –
> stepped back to note the effect – added a touch here and
> there – criticised the effect again – Ben watching every
> move and getting more and more interested, more and
> more absorbed. Presently he said: 'Say, Tom, let me
> whitewash a little.'

By the middle of the afternoon, the fence has three coats of
whitewash and Tom is literally rolling in wealth: one boy after
another has parted with his riches for the privilege of painting
a part of the fence. Tom has succeeded in 'reframing' drudgery
as a pleasure for which one has to pay, and all his friends, have
followed this change of his definition of reality.

When you reframe your negative experience to give it a new
meaning several things happen. First you find at least one way
in which the obstacle is actually an asset. Your slice in golf
is an obstacle until you use it to manoeuvre around a dogleg
fairway. A sales man comes to see his stammer as an asset when
he notices that it causes many people to listen more carefully to
his words than they do to a slicker but, intrusive, sales pitch.

Part of the initial confusion about the technique arises from
your unconscious assumption that there is an objective reality
'out there' or that there is only 'one truth', only one meaning
to be given to each event. Yet the meaning a scratch golfer
gives to a round of 76 is very different than that given by an

8-handicap player! The difficulty is to disentangle the event
from the meaning you give to it. It is not unfair, cheating or
dishonest to reframe. It allows you to see things differently.

The second result of reframing is that the problem often
begins to dissipate or change. By reframing your slice in golf,
you pay less attention towards changing it and thereby reduce
the contributing anxiety, tension and faulty mental practices. In
a peculiar sort of way, by appreciating your slice more for what
it is, you make the problem less. Sometimes we recommend
that you actually 'do it more' – exaggerate the mistake, make
the problem bigger. In so doing you begin to exert control over
a function which had previously been controlling you.

Re-creation

Our concept of re-creation, the fourth stage in the process
of change, corresponds to most people's concept of change
itself. We call this stage re-creation because it involves you
're-creating' yourself. On the simplest level, you do this by
substituting new patterns for old. However re-creation is part
of a process. You don't just jump into new patterns hoping that
your old patterns will magically disappear.

Re-creation follows the previous three stages. New patterns
are like seedlings. Before you plant them you must prepare
the soil. You then cultivate, eliminating weeds and misplaced
plants that compete for light and space. You plan where you
will plant the seedlings. You plant them, water them, fertilise
and continue to cultivate them until they are established. If you
don't spend the time in preparation, the seedlings won't take or
will produce a poor crop.

In this process you are changing your old attitudes and
beliefs at a fundamental level, creating new ones about
yourself and your world. Beliefs and attitudes, as we said
earlier, are habits of mind. As such they can be changed,
but there are several important factors in creating such
change.

- You have to know the habit that you want to change

- You need to have clear alternatives to the habit you want to change

- You need to choose a time to begin disidentifying and changing the habit

- You need to have a strategy for implementing the new habit

- And, you need to practise implementing the new habit, pattern or belief, *regularly*

Synthesis

As you build new patterns of behaviour your old self-image begins to change and the process of change usually gains a momentum of its own. Yet the new patterns are not always what we thought they might be. They tend to grow and take form in a way which synthesises the best of the old and the new. If you were too aggressive before and you develop receptivity or gentleness, you may wake up one day to discover that you have become confident. If you have expressed yourself powerfully in your performance and you work on developing your skill you may end up embodying authority. A conflict between two parts, the part that needed recognition and the part that wanted to be independent, may gradually be transformed into a capacity to advise and counsel others.

As you start to move beyond patterns which you have had for years, you discover that you can live quite comfortably with contradiction and paradox. You may have two or more very different sides to your character which you express at different times and in different ways. Yet if you try to get rid of one part or another, you risk losing the positive quality inherent in that part, or you find it breaking out inappropriately to sabotage your best efforts when you least expect it.

You have to remember that there is no end state. Change is

constant. As you begin to actualise your Vision and achieve your goals, other horizons will appear. Part of learning to accept and cultivate your potential is the ability to accept change as well.

There are many different processes and mental training exercises which can help you to embody your potential. Some, such as the use of symbols and positive affirmations, continue the deepening process of change. Others work at helping you to reconcile apparent contradictions. Still others attempt to bridge the gap between unexpressed potential and apparent shortcomings, making it possible to jump straight from understanding the problem to an insight or action which embodies the new.

There are six basic principles that lie behind many of our mental training exercises and which belong to this final step of the change process. The first two provide a basis for reducing obstacles to your progress, the rest provide a basis for reinforcing your strengths.

Win/win

Responding creatively to competition, you see the opportunity it provides to discover your potential, rather than struggle to match some pre-determined view of yourself. If your Vision or part way objective involves working within a team where you must compete on some issue with a *colleague*, you may need to reframe competition to discover the creative elements of the situation.

To reach synthesis, you then consider: 'What would it be like if we could *both* be winners?' This allows you to create a relationship where you may both fulfil your potential. It asks you to step out of your adversarial pattern and see yourself as part of a greater whole, connected with those with whom you have to compete. Competition then becomes creative not just for yourself but for your team mate and the team as a whole.

Bottom up

Years of experience working with clients have confirmed a basic conviction on our part: people are wiser than they realise! You may not always be fully conscious of where you want to go or how to get there but your essential self often knows. When you begin to work with your Vision, you open doors to another level of understanding. As you reach towards your potential it seems that you can count on your inner wisdom to find the way to achieve it. The main challenge seems to be getting out of its way.

Our primary 'bottom up' exercise is the visualisation in which you take your problem to the Wise Old Person at the top of the mountain (see p 157.). The Wise Old Person embodies some special place of understanding. The visualisation allows you access to knowledge hidden in your unconscious, which includes not only all your past experience but also your future potential. You know what is possible as well as what has already happened. Seeing the Wise Old Person allows you to use your unconscious to discover what needs to happen next. It is particularly good if you are blocked and don't know what to do when all else fails or when you are dealing with a particularly intractable part of yourself.

Top down

If you can take a problem 'up' in order to get a solution to it, you can also bring the good news down to the problematical situation. In a way, 'visioning' is a 'top down' process. You invite your future dream, your potential or who you might become to make itself known to you. Strategies are your plans for making that Vision real. But sometimes, as you act out your plan, the inspiration wears a bit thin. You may then need to invite your insight or inspiration back down to your daily life and activities. Don't plod on in a set routine following set plans to achieve set goals. Draw new energy and enthusiasm down into your performance.

Inspiration, intuition and insight all are top down experiences. They can be evoked in many ways. Start by referring back to your Vision. If you tied it down with a symbol, a badge, an emblem, a flag, a song or an ideal model, these things can lead you back into renewed understanding, energy, commitment and enthusiasm. Alternatively, go to see someone at the top of your field perform: attend an international match or a one-day business seminar with an inspirational presenter. Find the perfect image of the particular quality or action you want to develop and tap into it through association. In so doing you open yourself to the experience of a burst of energy for doing things in a new way.

Symbolisation

Symbolisation is a key technique for capturing potential and inspiration. Symbols and images are carriers of psychic energy. They are the language of the unconscious. They can pull together different strands of experience in a way which gives meaning to the diverse elements of that experience.

Symbols capture the new. They carry messages of a different kind, tightly encapsulated nuggets of meaning and non-verbal comprehension. Often they serve as vehicles for reconnecting with the inspiration of your Vision.

Symbolic actions capture the imagination and generate energy for change. You may paint out the reserved car spaces in your corporate parking lot. You may come into work before anyone else. You may train with the team instead of watching. You may share your technical knowledge with a team mate instead of keeping it to yourself. Symbolic actions carry a special message which is communicated and experienced in action rather than through talk. People know you mean it because you do it.

Positive thinking and positive doing

When it comes right down to it, positive thinking is often the simplest answer. Positive thinking is the most straightforward kind of substitution practice. Instead of asking you to practise being a certain way *vis-à-vis* mental rehearsal or symbolisation, it asks you to change your thinking directly. Positive thinking can be the most direct route to change although in some ways the most difficult.

It is the most direct because there are no intermediate steps. You simply think, feel or do what you desire to. It is difficult because there is no bridge between the old and the new. It's fine to have the intention but usually it also helps to know how to get from A to B. The strategies we've outlined in this chapter begin to address the 'how' of that process. The exercises most closely associated with the concept of positive thinking are affirmations and slogans.

Visioning

And so we return full circle. Building a Vision is a major step in synthesising a new view of yourself and the world. You begin to create a new reality: how you will be in the future, *now*. You jump straight to the core statement of your aspirations. You are the architect of your future life. As you set goals, you are drawing up the blueprint. As you evaluate what helps and hinders and assess your skills, you are organising the work crew and getting the materials ordered. Building the actual house corresponds to all the steps between: understanding, reframing, problem-solving, disidentifying, reowning, re-creating beliefs, modelling, synthesising and symbolisation. Proclaim your Vision again and again in as many ways as possible and see it come into being – your own World Trade Centre, your own St Paul's Cathedral, your own Taj Mahal. Finally you embody your Vision and become your potential.

12

Some case studies

Building a personal mental training programme ('thinking to win') is exciting and rewarding. Exciting because you begin to develop skills and assets you didn't realise you had. Rewarding because you begin to discover how you can create change in your life. These two processes combine to create a new self-image: you have hidden resources you never knew you had *and* the ability to consciously choose how you want to be.

The strategy used could be broken down into three fundamental stages.

1 **Where you're at** establishes where you're coming from and where you want to go. It's about creating a climate in which you have time to aspire to your full potential. This stage is the meeting of the past (what's so, resources, obstacles and self assessment) with the future (your Vision and your goals).

2 **Stopping the old** is probably the stage that most often gets left out. We are often in such a hurry to get to our destination that we forget the need to fully break with the past. It is not a long or complicated process, but it does need to be done. Otherwise the past will creep back on to the centre stage as soon as you turn your attention in another direction.

3 **Building the new** is the most exciting stage because it's the experience of embodying the new. It's based upon all the groundwork that went before. When you've cleared all of the undergrowth from the past which might get in the

way of living the new, you have created the best context for the future.

The best way to illustrate how we implement this strategy is through several case studies. They illustrate the many different tools and processes that have been used to enliven and energise the growth of the individual. None of the mental training programmes detailed demonstrate action plans which are complete. But no action plan is ever complete – if it were it would fail to take into account the fact that change is an on-going process.

We've also chosen examples of individuals who were faced with situations and problems which are relatively common: dealing with anxiety when faced with a top-level opponent; being called into a new situation with the remit to sort out a team which is not working; and making a major career move. In each case we'll follow through the six stages of our 'strategies for change'.

Case study 1

History

This individual was a top level British trap-shooter who competed on the European circuit. She was gifted and, like many athletes, competed effectively and competently when at home. She was outstanding in her natural ability but found that the pressure of European competition often did not draw out her best, although she was bored with the general level of competition that the British shooting scene offered. She came to us with a general remit to improve her performance and realise her full potential.

Goals

Angela's vision was twofold. She wanted to achieve the full realisation of her potential in her sport which she felt would be actualised by becoming the best in Europe. She also wanted to find a way to enjoy her sport and to be able to live in, or even better, thrive, in the competitive environment.

What's so

Resources :   A survey of Angela's resources showed that she had good and consistent techniques. She was highly skilful. She also had very good reflexes: she always caught the clay 'bird' very early in its flight and had plenty of time to take her second shot on the occasions that she missed. When she was on form she could beat anyone in Europe.

Obstacles: There was always the element of self-doubt when competing on the continent. This had initially to do with the fact that there was so much money invested in the facilities and the standard of competition was much higher. However, it had more to do with a loss of certainty or confidence in her skills when competing at international level. Against world-standard competitors she was inclined to turn in some of her worst scores. It was as if competing against the best sapped her confidence and lowered her self-esteem. This was particularly reinforced when she competed against the world champion. It resulted in increased anxiety and a decline in performance. It was this main obstacle which kept her from using her innate ability to achieve her goal of becoming European champion.

Disidentification

The disidentification process involved highlighting her main conflicting polarity: On the one hand she was extrememly fast and highly proficient technically. On the other hand she let self-doubt creep in and undermine her natural ability. Angela engaged in a series of dialogues with the conflicting parts and began to see that while she had both of these patterns or ways of responding to the competitive situation she was not one or the other. These were behaviour patterns which emerged at different times and under different circumstances.

Reframing

Reframing in this situation involved a reexamination of competing with the world champion, Bridget. Two things were discovered. Firstly, she didn't perform well in these head-on competitions against Bridget because she felt very nervous. Her lack of calm was initially perceived as a handicap. But this assumption was challenged. Was the actual physical state of anxiety bad or was only the meaning attributed to it bad? Could anxiety be experienced as excitement if she perceived the situation differently? In fact, when reviewing her most successful competitions she felt confident *and* excited. She felt good about herself and the situation and, as a result, enjoyed the excitement of the competition. Viewed from a different perspective anxiety became excitement!

Secondly, when she described her opponent she discovered that in fact they had a lot in common. Bridget was skilful, extremely solid technically and very quick. The main difference was that under the strain of competition she seemed to become more solid, consistent and focused. So Angela discovered that in terms of ability and skill she was very much like her opponent. Before she had focused on their differences very much to her own detriment. It was almost as if Angela gave away to Bridget all of her own skill and resources. She could see them in her opponent but not in herself.

Re-creation

The particular mental exercise we used to deal with this situation was **turning anxiety into energy**. Angela practised a visualisation of herself competing against Bridget in which she saw all the power, control, skill and natural ability of her opponent focused on her own range. Angela then imagined that there was an arc of light like a rainbow, between herself and her opponent and, as they shot, she could see this light act as a bridge or conduit for all of the talent and ability she had been projecting on to Bridget. Angela visualised the energy flowing into her from Bridget and as she did so she felt herself growing in ability, talent, quick reflexes and skill. She was reowning her projection, in this case a positive one, and beginning to reconnect with the very resources she knew she had but seemed to have given away to her opponent. She became stronger, clearer, more proficient and more competitive.

The result was a consistent improvement in her performance, increased comfort during competition and a renewed joy in her own abilities. She also experienced an enhanced self-esteem as she discovered that she could muster her abilities when and where she needed them and a growing self-respect as she became more and more respected on the European circuit.

Synthesis

Angela won the European Championships that year. She performed at a high level throughout Europe. She began to look forward with great anticipation to her continental trips, where she performed at a consistently high level and built many friendships throughout the European circuit. The new synthesis took two main forms. Firstly she discovered that she could now enjoy competition and that the old anxiety states were increasingly supplanted by a sense of well-being and pleasure. Secondly, she discovered that many of the other tasks she performed in her daily life to do with her business and profession also became easier. She had more time, she could concentrate better, she seemed more focused and competent. She was generally more relaxed, she enjoyed showing off her skills and could accept the high regard in which she was held by her peers. Mental training and development in her sport led to increased performance and well-being in other areas of her life.

Case study 2

History

Bill had recently been appointed to take over as department head of a division within his company. This department had had a difficult few years. Its role was shrinking within the company and there was much concern about job security. Cliques and subgroups within the management team had formed, all of whom thought that they were working for the best of the department. As a consequence, there was confusion, rumours and general discontent amongst the lower grades of the department and also amongst the hourly-paid workers.

Goals

Bill had come from a larger but less controversial department. His real ambition had always been to build an enthusiastic and happy team. He wanted team members to work together and support each other. He was keen that his team should be both efficient and happy. In order to achieve this he also knew that he needed to evoke both loyalty and trust.

What's so

Resources: Bill had the experience of working for a boss who had embodied much of what he aspired to in management. He had come from a department where the team spirit was high and there was a shared sense of responsibility and enthusiasm for the job. He had an 'ideal model' in the form of his previous boss and knew how a happy successful team should feel and act. He also had the ability to listen to people who didn't agree with him. He could see their strengths, even if they were being used against the best interests of the department or indeed against him. So he was a good judge of character and was not personally attached to being liked or disliked. He could differentiate easily between what was really him and what were other people's projections. In addition, Bill had a sense of humour. His Vision encompassed a department which had fun together and could joke with each other without planting hidden barbs in the jokes.

Obstacles: His obstacles were both external and internal. Externally the department had expected someone to be promoted from within and they were disappointed that Bill had been brought in from outside. Consequently there was some resentment from the management team and in particular from the two team members who felt that they should have been given a shot at the job. Secondly, even though the old management style hadn't necessarily built a really solid team, everyone was used to being their own boss. They had been given free rein to use whatever management style and approach suited them as long as they got the job done. On the one hand this promoted a sense of autonomy and freedom, on the other there was no consistent management style and approach which set the tone for the whole department.

'Internally', Bill was unsure of his ability to act as a peacemaker when what he really needed to do was get on with the job. He was used to listening to people but also to taking decisions. He wasn't sure he had the patience or skill to sort out past problems and the truth was that he would have rather been getting on with the necessary steps for planning the future. Secondly, it was a new part of the company for him so he was unsure of his command of the field. Many of his team knew more than he did about the operation. He needed their support but was uncertain if he could ask for their support without giving away his own authority.

Disidentification

The key disidentification process involved a series of chair dialogues with his former boss. This boss became an ideal model for him and in the exercise he put the memory or image of his old boss on an empty chair and asked his advice. This ideal model acted as an internalised reservoir of experience, held in the unconscious until it needed to be drawn out through this exercise. For him it was experienced as a realisation that he wasn't stuck in the situation on his own. He had 'hidden' extra resources and could call on his boss's experience even if he couldn't talk to the old boss. He also realised that he wasn't stuck in the situation. He could step outside of it into his 'external observer'.

Reframing

The key reframing of the situation came when he realised that in fact he had a loyal team. Up until this point, he had thought of the team as being essentially martialled against him in favour of their old boss. He reframed this by recognising that in fact the team was very loyal: they were loyal to the old head of department, reserving their loyalty and respect while they decided if Bill was worthy of it. Bill realised that the team wasn't disloyal, it was simply not yet loyal to him. His task then became how to shift their loyalty from the past to the present, in many ways a simpler task than trying to build loyalty out of nothing.

The second reframing came about when we began to organise a plan for developing the loyalty of the team. Up until this point Bill had seen it as his sole responsibility to institute the change. He had felt he had to do it all. We pointed out that he could just as easily make it the joint responsibility of the team to institute the change. In fact he could avoid a lot of the conflict by confronting the issue directly: 'How are *we* going to make the new team work? Who amongst the management team is going to take responsibility for bringing me up to date? How are we going to work together as a team?'

Re-creation

In terms of reinforcing the positive, we built heavily on Bill's old boss. He became an ideal model and Bill practised ideal model visualisations in which he mentally rehearsed being his old boss. How did this boss feel, act, respond to similar situations in the past? How would he respond to the current situation? We then suggested that Bill act 'As If': actually speaking and acting as his old boss would. Bill was also a keen golfer and we used another ideal, Jack Nicklaus, as a model. Bill had always admired Nicklaus' composure on the course and so he began to conduct his management meetings *as if* he were Jack Nicklaus. This brought out a new dimension to his personality and his management team experienced him as unflappable and collected during the contentiousness of early management meetings. They quickly dropped their challenging mode: they were more interested in finding out what he was thinking. Bill had an autographed picture of Jack Nicklaus which he put on his desk. When he came in each morning and throughout the day he could key in, through the photo, to the qualities he was cultivating in his team-leading performance.

On the interpersonal level, we asked him to apply the same reframing of the loyalty issue to the individuals who were passed over when he was assigned the job. We led several 'pairs sessions' between Bill and each of his senior managers in turn. In these, Bill and the manager with whom he was paired each completed a number of sentences along the lines of 'I appreciate you when . . .', 'What I need most from you is . . .', 'I feel distanced from you when . . .', 'Our strength as a unit is . . .', etc.

He then drew upon their advice, regularly asking for their candid opinions. Rather than trying to cut off the power base of these individuals who had a great deal of potential and could sabotage his Vision for the department, Bill included them in many of his key decision-making sessions and won them over to his side. Again he assumed that they were loyal and had only to learn how to be loyal to him. He also asked them how to structure the internal organisation so that the other management team members still had their accustomed freedom while making greater demands upon their accountability.

Synthesis

The synthesis came about when he asked the team to develop their new Vision of the department. He asked the management team to organise a small Vision group which would meet regularly to formulate a departmental Vision with the proviso that they report back to him. It was time for the department to develop a new self-image and a new Vision – but one that was based upon the future not the past. In so doing, he little by little began to focus the attention of the entire department on where they were going instead of where they had come from. Rather than trying to crush or block the old, he simply began to implement a new direction and Vision for the future, for which members of the department were equally responsible. Because they were involved in building this Vision, their loyalty to the old was slowly transferred to the Vision for the new. Bill was seen as a part of that Vision and the loyalty was soon transferred to him as well. The capstone to the Vision was the departmental tune. When he heard it being whistled in the lavatory, he knew that he had made it.

Case study 3

History

Ellen was a housewife in her early 40s whose children had grown up. She wanted to reenter the business world. It was a classic situation of a wife who gave up her career ambitions to raise a family and now found that she was no longer satisfied with the role she was playing. She had had experience managing a small business during the early years of her marriage and was ready to do it again. Her university education was in art history and she was keen to open a small silkscreen and printing business which would provide a service to young art school graduates and yet also cater to designers and publishers.

Goals

Ellen's Vision was twofold. She wanted to provide a service

which was special: she wanted to be commercially viable (not just have it be a play fantasy as her husband was inclined to view it) and yet to be involved in the mainstream of the artistic community rather than the more humdrum side of reproductions. The second part of her Vision involved her personal aspiration to be creative, autonomous and self-supporting. For her, the need to rediscover her ability to be effective in the world outside of her family environment had become crucial.

What's so

Resources: Ellen had had considerable exposure through her university education to the arts of etching, silkscreening and printmaking. She had a trained eye and had often been able to spot rising talent when she continued to view showings and openings during her years as a housewife

She had also run a fairly large house and had organised a number of very efficient household systems. These had kept all of her family happy and well looked after while allowing her to continue her involvement in the world of art.

She knew how to make things work. She was strong, physically and mentally, had a lot of stamina and was willing to put in long hours.

Obstacles: Ellen's obstacles were internal and external. Internally her main problem was a sense of insecurity and a lack of experience. She had 'bought into' the idea of 'a woman's role is in the home' and questioned her own ability to actually maintain a high profile in the art world which had become considerably more competitive since she had experienced it in her 20s. While she had managed a shop during her early years of marriage, the commercial side of printing was unknown to her. She knew it was not an easy area to break into.

Externally, her biggest problem was her family. They weren't really supporting her, either because they thought her Vision was a whim or because they saw it as involving her in a lot of work and time commitments which would reduce their access to her.

Disidentification

The main challenge before creating the new was to deal with all of the negative introjections she had taken on over the years, around her capacity as a business woman and her role outside of the family. She had developed a very strong subpersonality whom she called 'Doubting Thomas' who never really believed that she would be able to handle the additional responsibility. In an important session she took this subpersonality up the mountain to meet her Wise Old Person. Here, to her surprise, she discovered that her Doubting Thomas also had a tremendous ability to discriminate between 'the genuine article' and what was false or second rate.

Her Wise Old Person suggested that she use this critical facility for deciding which artists she choose to print and which dealers she approached. She realised that she could save herself a tremendous amount of despair and energy if she applied this facility to those people and situations she encountered rather than attacking herself. She made a contract with Doubting Thomas that whenever she found herself attacking her own self-esteem, she would took around for a task or project that needed a decision and apply that same critical eye to the problem.

Interestingly, it was also this session which gave her another key for reframing when she realised that her Doubting Thomas never doubted her judgement when it came to running her household.

Reframing

Ellen's reframing took in both her obstacles and her resources. With her obstacles she very quickly realised that her family's impressions of her ability was very strongly determined by their desire for her not to leave the home. She could see that their image of her bore very little resemblance to who she actually was. She began to recognise that other people had attitudes which influenced how they thought and that she could disentangle herself from these attitudes. One way of doing this was through a simple thought-stopping technique. When she recognised that family and friends were holding a certain thought-form about her, she simply repeated to herself: 'I see that Joe views me as a housewife and these are not my views. I have the ability to be a housewife *and* I am more than a housewife.' She used this process repeatedly: 'Those are someone else's views. I may have that ability and I am more than that ability or the views of others.'

Ellen also reframed her experience as a housewife. Her inclination had been to focus on all the aspects of her experience other than being a housewife. But in fact, this one was the key. Her past experience suddenly became an asset instead of a hindrance. She had massive amounts of experience organising resources, keeping accounts, keeping the family fed, organising transport: all the skills generally needed for running a small business. A liability came to be seen as an asset and time and energy which might have been spent trying to erase the past experience was suddenly available for focusing on the skills which she did need to develop.

Re-creation

Having reframed her home experience and transformed it into an asset, Ellen practised a number of mental rehearsals in which she revisited all the times in her career as a housewife when she demonstrated clarity, strength, the ability to organise, diplomacy and discrimination. Then in the mental rehearsal she imagined stepping out of the home, walking into her printing studio and applying the same qualities and skills. Very rapidly Ellen began to discover just how many of her homemaker skills she could use in the work situation. Instead of trying to block out her housewife experience, it was used and salvaged, the very best of it being taken and applied in her job to make this new situation work. She lost very little of her past, reowned it and became proud of her experience as a housewife. She also short-cut a lot of worry and unnecessary time she had allocated to 'retraining' by using her 'resource management' skills in a business situation.

Ellen got a symbol for the key qualities of her new attitude – a mountain which represented the unshakeable courage of her convictions. She decided to use this symbol for her business and put it on her stationery. The original photograph from which the mountain was drawn was blown up and hung in the entrance of her studio so she and everyone saw it each time they walked in.

For her family, Ellen used visual re-editing. Whenever she had an encounter in which they expressed doubt or criticism and she ended up having an argument with them, Ellen would use a visual re-editing technique. She would go back to the occasion in her mind, play it through and then edit her own role in the scene so that rather than feeling attacked or aggressive she saw herself as acting cool, calm and collected, responding caringly and yet firmly. The family soon stopped attacking her as they became aware of her new confidence and imperturbability. Ellen experienced that she had the choice to respond differently to her family than the way in which they unconsciously wanted her to and she suddenly saw herself breaking out of the old thought-form that both they and she had held about herself.

Synthesis

The synthesis emerged surprisingly in a personal affirmation which became the motto of her company: 'I hold the best of my past as the key to my future' eventually became 'The traditional methods of the past used to unlock the potential of the future.' In addition Ellen created an environment at her studio which was homely and comfortable. Staff, artists, dealers and friends enjoyed being welcomed and nurtured. It was this mixture of the competency and efficiency of her systems combined with the homeliness of her studio which drew repeat orders and rapidly made her business a notable success.